Boutique Bags

Classic Style *for* Modern Living

19 Projects • 76 Bags

Sue Kim

stash BOOKS®
an imprint of C&T Publishing

Text and photography copyright © 2015 by Sue Kim

Photography and artwork copyright © 2015 by C&T Publishing, Inc.

Publisher: Amy Marson

Creative Director: Gailen Runge

Art Director: Kristy Zacharias

Editor: Liz Aneloski

Technical Editors: Debbie Rodgers and Julie Waldman

Cover/Book Designer: April Mostek

Production Coordinators: Jenny Davis and Rue Flaherty

Production Editor: Katie Van Amburg

Illustrator: Zinnia Heinzmann

Photo Assistant: Mary Peyton Peppo

Style photography by Nissa Brehmer; Gallery photography by Diane Pedersen; How-to photography by Sue Kim, unless otherwise noted

Published by Stash Books, an imprint of C&T Publishing, Inc., P.O. Box 1456, Lafayette, CA 94549

Library of Congress Cataloging-in-Publication Data

Kim, Sue, 1969-

  Boutique bags : classic style for modern living - 19 projects 76 bags / Sue Kim.

    pages cm

  ISBN 978-1-60705-985-1 (soft cover)

  1. Handbags. I. Title.

TT667.K5225 2015

646.4'8--dc23

                    2014038488

Printed in China

10 9 8 7 6 5 4 3 2 1

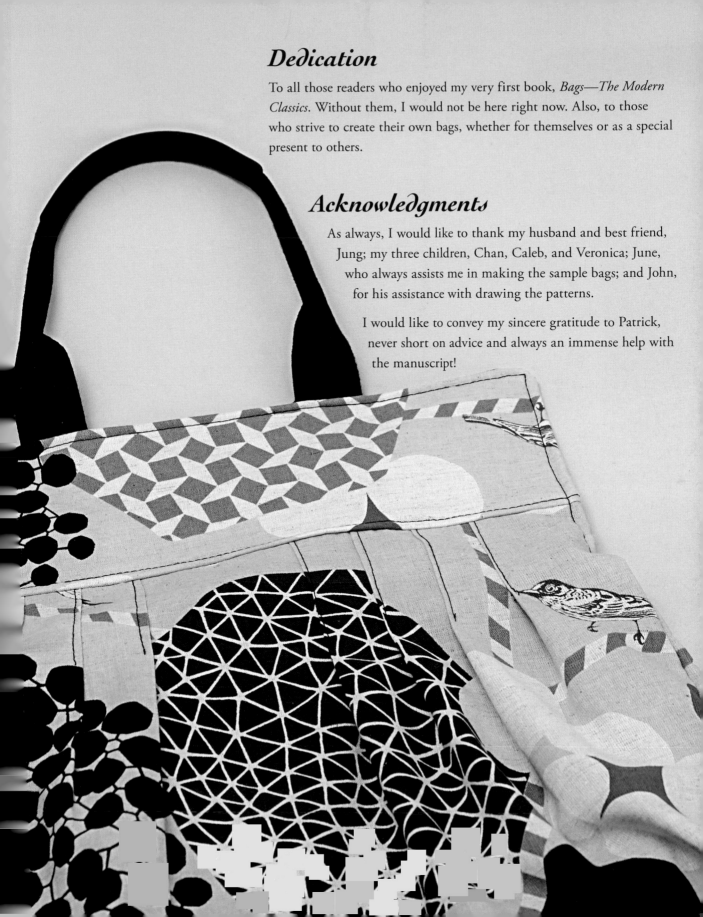

Dedication

To all those readers who enjoyed my very first book, *Bags—The Modern Classics*. Without them, I would not be here right now. Also, to those who strive to create their own bags, whether for themselves or as a special present to others.

Acknowledgments

As always, I would like to thank my husband and best friend, Jung; my three children, Chan, Caleb, and Veronica; June, who always assists me in making the sample bags; and John, for his assistance with drawing the patterns.

I would like to convey my sincere gratitude to Patrick, never short on advice and always an immense help with the manuscript!

Table of Contents

Introduction 6

Tools, Supplies, and Basic Techniques 7

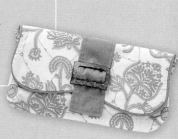

SMALL PROJECTS

Gathered Zipper Pouches 20

Madison Metal Purse
and Coin Case 28

CLUTCHES

Jayleen Clutch 34

Evelyn Clutch 44

BAGS

Julianna Bag 50

Linnea Ruffled Bag 56

Genevieve Ruffled Bag 62

Thelma Bag 70

Susan Boston Bag 76

Violet Bag 84

Valentina Bag 90

June Big Bag 96

Miranda Bag 104

Stephanie Bag 110

Market Bag and Pouch 116

Gallery 124

Resources 127

About the Author 127

Introduction

I wrote my first book, *Bags—The Modern Classics*, with beginning-level sewists in mind, so I kept the supplies to a minimum. This new book still includes many projects that are achievable for beginning sewists, but it also includes a few more intricate designs that use various types of materials including metal frames, leather handles, buckles, and so on.

My goal is to help you gain confidence in your sewing skills and take the next step forward.

Tools, Supplies, and Basic Techniques

Tools and Supplies

You will need a few basic tools and supplies: sewing machine, all-purpose sewing thread, hand and machine needles, pincushion, ruler, safety pins, straight pins, scissors, seam ripper, pattern weights, measuring tape, and chalk; a serger is a nice bonus but not mandatory.

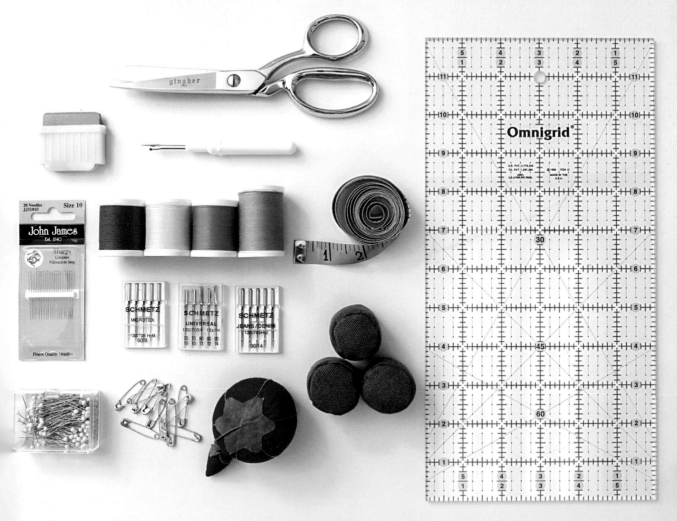

I use linen, cotton, home decor fabric, quilting-weight cotton, faux fur, and waterproof fabric for the exterior fabric and quilting-weight cotton for lining. I use light- to medium-weight interfacing, depending on the weight of the bag fabric. I use roll zippers, so I can trim to any length I need!

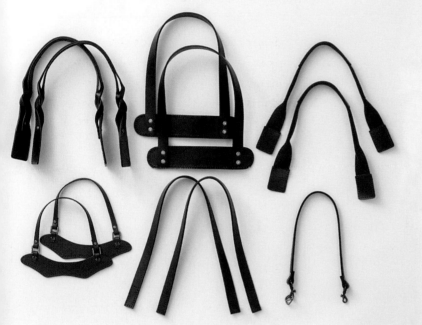

There are several different kinds of leather handles available to suit your bag's design. Some include pre-punched holes so you can sew on the handles after completing the bag. Other options include O-ring or D-ring attachment varieties. Find the perfect handle for your bag and make it!

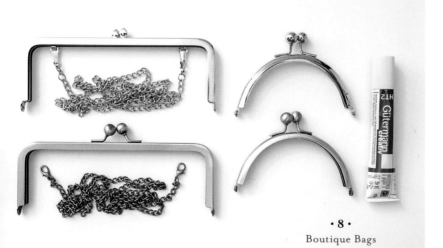

Some metal purse frames include an attached chain to utilize it as a handbag style. Others have a detachable chain, for optional use. The fabric edge of the bag is glued into the channel of the frame, so even beginners will have a fun time using this frame!

Basic Techniques

Applying a Magnetic Snap

Attach the magnetic snap following the manufacturer's instructions.
Most snaps attach with the following steps:

1. Cut a small piece of fusible interfacing at least ¼" larger on all sides than the snap.

2. Apply the interfacing to the wrong side of the fabric, centered on the snap location.

3. Center the snap on the piece of interfacing. **FIGURE A**

4. Use a pencil to draw the lines on the fabric where it will need to be cut for the prongs.

5. Mark and carefully snip the slits for the prongs. **FIGURE B**

6. Insert the prongs of a magnet on the right side of the fabric. **FIGURE C**

7. Place the disk over the prongs on the wrong side of the fabric and fold the prongs outward over the disc. Finish by attaching the other half of the magnetic snap on the other piece in the same manner. **FIGURE D**

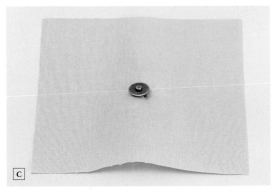

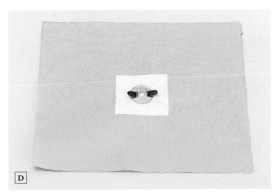

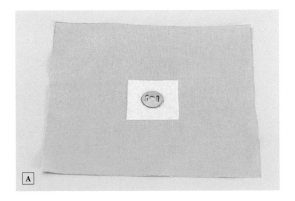

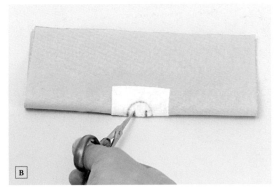

Attaching an O-Ring

1. Cut 2 pieces of ribbon each 2″ long. Press both short edges of a piece of ribbon under ⅜″. **FIGURE E**

2. Press the ribbon in half. Slip the O-ring onto the ribbon. Stitch the ribbon ends together. **FIGURE F**

3. Position the ribbon on the side seam of the lining. Pin in place and stitch. **FIGURE G**

4. Repeat Steps 1–3 for the other ribbon O-ring holder.

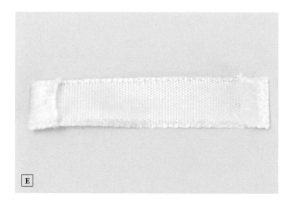

E

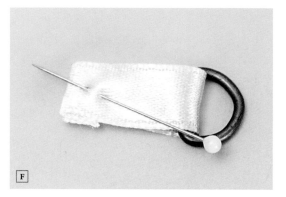

F

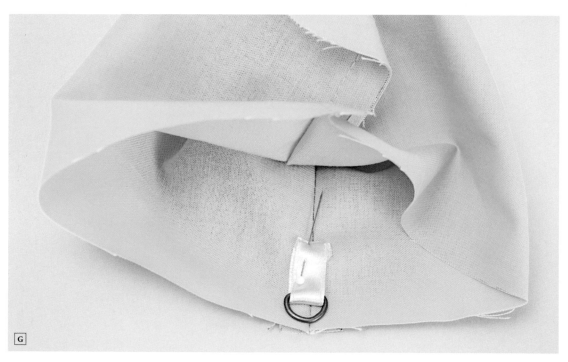

G

Attaching a Twist Lock

1. Using a screwdriver, disassemble the lock.

2. Place the back piece onto the lining flap.

3. Trace the back piece onto the lining. **FIGURE H**

4. Cut out the center area of the back piece on the flap; punch the screw holes on each side with an awl or the tip of the scissors. **FIGURE I**

5. Lay the front lock piece onto the exterior, match the back lock piece with the front, and then screw them together. **FIGURE J**

6. Draw the cutting line onto the front clutch piece as provided on the pattern. **FIGURE K**

7. Insert the lock piece, place the washer onto the prongs, and fold the prongs outward. If you would like, you can add a piece of interfacing to stabilize the lock. **FIGURE L**

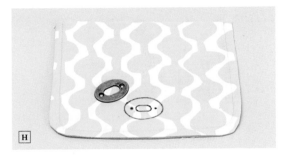

H

I

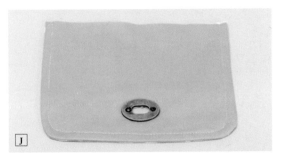

J

K

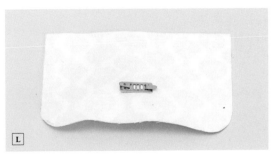

L

Clipping and Trimming a Seam

CLIPPING

Making small V-shaped cuts on the inner (concave seams) or outer (convex seams) curves help them lie flat when turned to the right side. Always notch within the seam allowance, not beyond it. **FIGURE M**

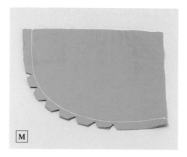

TRIMMING

With the piece wrong side out, trim off the excess fabric at the corners to reduce the bulk and create a nice, sharp corner when you turn the piece right side out. **FIGURE N**

Pockets

A variety of pockets are used in the bag projects.

STANDARD POCKET

1. Position the pocket pattern onto the right side of the pocket fabric. Cut 2.

2. Sew the pocket with right sides together, leaving a side open for turning. Trim the corners. See Trimming (above). **FIGURE O**

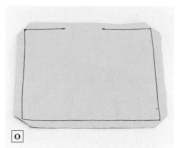

3. Turn the pocket right side out and use a sharp tool to push the corners out.

4. Fold the seam allowances of the opening to the inside and press the pocket.

5. Pin the opening and topstitch ⅛″ from the opening side, backstitching on both ends. **FIGURE P**

6. Place the pocket on the right side of the lining as desired, or where indicated on the pattern. Topstitch the pocket in place, starting at the top of 1 side, sewing across the bottom and back up to the top, and backstitching at both ends. **FIGURE Q**

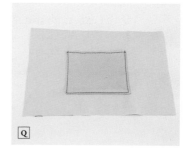

ELASTIC POCKET

1. To create the casing for the elastic, double-fold the top edge of the fabric piece ½". **FIGURE R**

2. Pin and sew along the bottom edge of the fold line, backstitching on both ends.

3. Attach a safety pin to an end of the elastic.

4. Insert the safety pin into an open end of the casing. **FIGURE S**

5. Work the safety pin through the length of the casing, stopping to stitch the end of the elastic within the seamline at the entry edge. Continue to work the safety pin through the casing and pull it out the open end, adjusting the gathers. Stitch the second end to secure the elastic. **FIGURE T**

6. Sew gathers along the bottom edge of the pocket. See Making Gathers (page 17). **FIGURE U**

7. Place the pocket piece on the lining back piece. The right side of the lining piece will meet the wrong side of the pocket. Pin along the bottom edge, making sure to pin at each end of the gathering thread. Pull an end of the running stitch thread. Pull the other end of the running stitch thread to match the length of the bottom of the lining back piece. Adjust the gathers and pin.

8. Adjust the length of the elastic to match the lining. Pin.

9. Sew the pocket to the lining, backstitching on both ends. Trim off the excess elastic.

10. Sew the pocket's divider lines at your desired intervals.
    FIGURE V

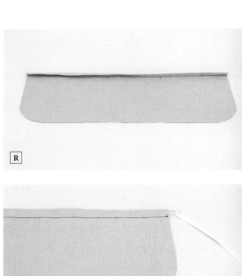

ZIPPER POCKET

1. Draw the zipper rectangle ⅜″ wide and 1″ shorter than the finished length of your zipper, as marked on the pattern, onto a pocket piece 1″ below the top edge. Place the zipper pocket piece onto the lining with right sides together. Stitch the rectangle on the line. **FIGURE W**

2. Cut down the center and to each corner, as marked on the zipper pocket pattern. **FIGURE X**

3. Fold the fabric toward the lining. **FIGURE Y**

4. Press the seam. The right side of the lining will look like the picture. **FIGURE Z**

5. Place the zipper onto the wrong side of the lining. Match the right side of the zipper with the wrong side of the lining. Stitch the zipper in place close to the folded edge of the fabric, backstitching at each end. **FIGURE AA**

6. Place the other zipper pocket piece right sides together to the first piece. Without stitching the lining, stitch the 2 pocket pieces together ⅜″ from the edge. **FIGURE BB**

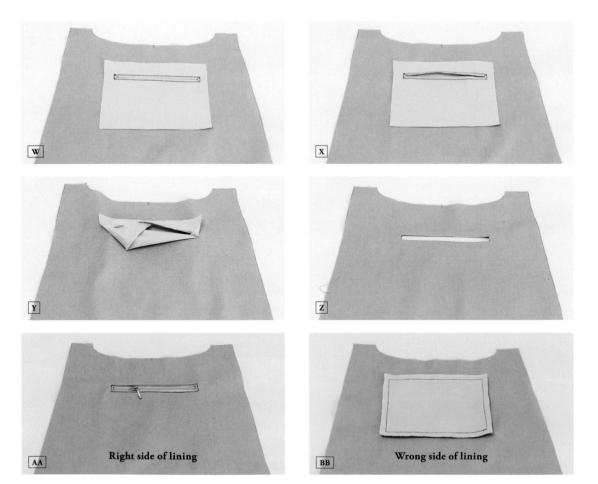

W

X

Y

Z

AA **Right side of lining**

BB **Wrong side of lining**

Attaching Piping

1. Leaving the first 1″–2″ of your piping unstitched, stitch the piping onto your fabric, aligning the long raw edges.

2. Stop stitching when you are 3″–4″ from the end of the piping and backstitch.

3. Trim off the excess piping, leaving about 1″ of overlap with the beginning end of the piping.

4. Remove a few of the original piping stitches at the second end of the piping and trim off about ½″ of the inner core of the piping.

5. Fold the short raw edge in ¼″ to the wrong side and finger-press the fold. **FIGURE CC**

6. Place the first end of the piping on the folded second end. Pin and sew to finish. **FIGURE DD**

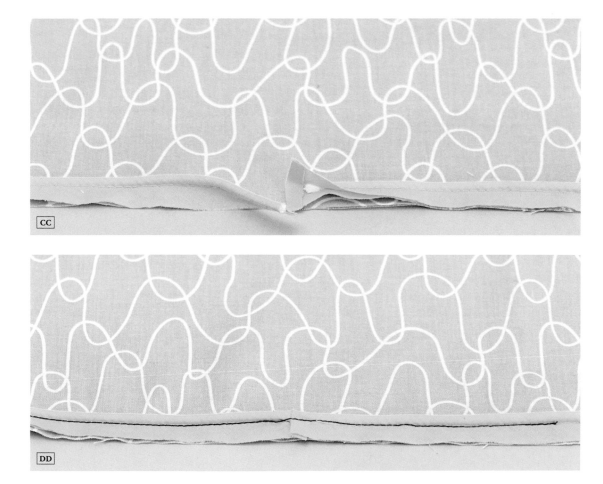

CC

DD

Installing a Metal Frame

1. Glue the purse and metal frame together by first applying fabric glue on the edge of the purse. **FIGURE EE**

2. Also apply fabric glue in the channel of the metal frame, from 1 hinge to the other, making sure that it doesn't overflow onto the fabric. **FIGURE FF**

3. Using a sharp tool, such as a pair of scissors, poke the purse into the frame. Start at the hinges and work your way through. Before inserting the paper cord, let the purse dry for about 20 minutes or until the metal frame is secure. **FIGURE GG**

4. Tuck the paper cord into the space between the fabric and frame with a sharp tool. **FIGURE HH**

5. Press the frame with a crimping tool. **FIGURE II**

> **NOTE**
>
> Be sure to place fabric between the tool and the metal frame so the frame doesn't become dented. Use a block-shaped crimping tool rather than a needle-nose crimping tool. Needle-nose ones will dent and scratch the frame rather than bend it to fit the purse.

You can use your purse as soon as the glue is completely dry, usually within a day.

EE

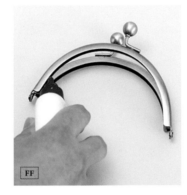
FF

GG

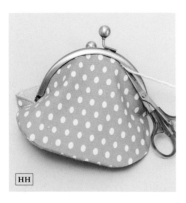
HH

II

Making Gathers

1. Sew 2 rows of hand or machine basting stitches on the fabric, within the seam allowance, as marked on the pattern. Leave a few inches of thread at each end. **FIGURE JJ**

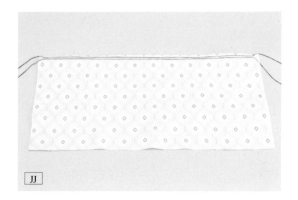

2. Pin at each end of the gathering stitches and wind the threads around the first pin in a figure-eight shape. Gently pull the threads at the other end until the gathered piece has been shortened to match the piece it will be sewn to, or to the length specified in the pattern. **FIGURE KK**

3. Wind these threads around the second pin in the same manner and spread the gathers evenly.

Sewing Darts

1. Lay the exterior front piece wrong side up. Fold the dart right sides together, matching the dart lines. Pin and stitch along the dart lines, backstitching at the beginning and end. **FIGURE LL**

2. Press the darts away from the center of the bag.

3. Stitch the back darts in the same manner, but press them toward the center of the bag. **FIGURE MM**

Sewing a Leather and Webbing Handle

1. Place the handle on the exterior of the bag at the desired location. Sew the handle to the bag with a running stitch, bringing the needle up in the first hole, down into the second hole, and up into the third. Continue in this fashion. **FIGURE NN**

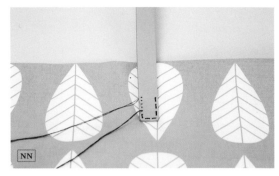

2. When you reach the end, continue the running stitch over the handle a second time, this time reversing the stitches so the thread fills the space between each pair of holes. **FIGURE OO**

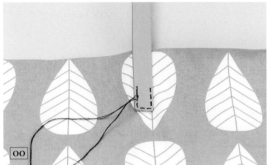

Stitching the Strap

STRAP A

1. Fold the strap in half lengthwise, wrong sides together, and press to make a crease. **FIGURE PP**

2. Open the strap with the wrong side facing you. Fold in each long side of the strap to the center crease and press. **FIGURE QQ**

3. Fold in half again along the first crease, press, and pin. Topstitch ⅛″ from the double-folded edge. **FIGURE RR**

STRAP B

1. Fold 1 end of the strap in ⅜″ and press. **FIGURE SS**

2. Fold the strap in half lengthwise, with the wrong sides together, and press to make a crease.

3. Open the strap with the wrong side facing you. Fold in each side of the strap to the center crease and press.

4. Fold in half again along the first crease and press. Topstitch ⅛″ from the double-folded edge.

Connecting an Adjustable Buckle

1. Slip a D-ring or O-ring onto the loop piece. Fold the loop over the ring and baste. **FIGURE TT**

2. Add the strap piece onto the adjustable buckle. **FIGURE UU**

3. Add the lobster lock onto the end of the strap. **FIGURE VV**

4. Fold the strap end back and insert it into the back side of the adjustable buckle. **FIGURE WW**

5. Fold the end of the strap over the center of the buckle and sew the 2 layers together without sewing the bottom, adjustable strap piece.

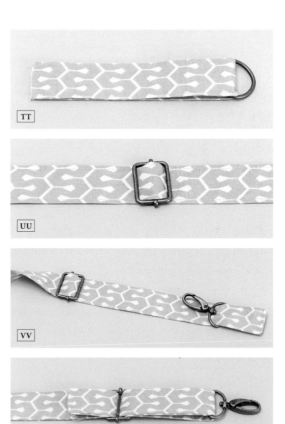

Tools, Supplies, and Basic Techniques

Gathered Zipper Pouches

With their defining gathers, these Gathered Zipper Pouches are a simple set that has an easy process of adding the zippers. The gathers not only add beauty to the pattern but they are practical by giving the pouch more storage room. With a few of these pouches inside your purse, you'll have an organized and convenient carry-around companion! You can also add a loop as a handle for easier carrying.

All three pouches can be made with the same fabric or with three different fabrics—the options are endless! This is also the perfect gift set.

FINISHED SIZES

Large: 13½" wide × 5" high × 2½" deep
Medium: 12" wide × 4" high × 2½" deep
Small: 9½" wide × 4" high × 2½" deep

SKILL LEVEL Confident Beginner ❈ ❈

MATERIALS

Amounts are based on 42"-wide fabric and are for 3 pouches (1 of each size).

¾ yard for exterior

¾ yard for lining

1¼ yards of fusible interfacing

10" all-purpose zipper for large

9" all-purpose zipper for medium

7" all-purpose zipper for small

NOTE

- A ⅜" seam allowance is included on the pattern.

- Backstitch at the beginning and end of each seam.

Gathered Zipper Pouches

CUTTING

Cut out the exterior, lining, and interfacing pieces as listed below.

Large Pouch ....

Exterior

- 2 pieces 10¼″ × 2⅛″ for Front/Back Top Panel
- 2 pieces 19″ × 6¼″ for Large Pouch Panel
- 1 piece 19″ × 1¾″ for wrist strap (*optional*)

Lining

- 2 pieces 10¼″ × 2⅛″ for Front/Back Top Panel
- 2 pieces 19″ × 6¼″ for Large Pouch Panel

Interfacing

- 2 pieces 10¼″ × 2⅛″ for Front/Back Top Panel
- 2 pieces 19″ × 6¼″ for Large Pouch Panel

Refer to the Large Pouch Panel diagram below to trace and trim the bottom corners of all the Large Pouch panels using the Gathered Zipper Pouches Corner (Large) pattern (pullout page P1).

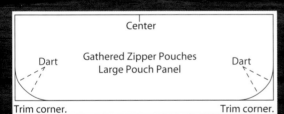

Medium Pouch ....

Exterior

- 2 pieces 9¾″ × 1¾″ for Front/Back Top Panel
- 2 pieces 18″ × 4⅞″ for Medium Pouch Panel
- 1 piece 19″ × 1¾″ for wrist strap (*optional*)

Lining

- 2 pieces 9¾″ × 1¾″ for Front/Back Top Panel
- 2 pieces 18″ × 4⅞″ for Medium Pouch Panel

Interfacing

- 2 pieces 9¾″ × 1¾″ for Front/Back Top Panel
- 2 pieces 18″ × 4⅞″ for Medium Pouch Panel

Refer to the Medium Pouch Panel diagram below to trace and trim the bottom corners of all the Medium Pouch Panels using the Gathered Zipper Pouches Corner (Medium) pattern (pullout page P1).

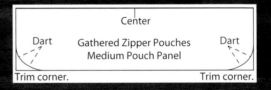

Small Pouch

Exterior

- 2 pieces 7¾" × 1¾" for Front/Back Top Panel

- 2 pieces 14¾" × 4⅞" for Small Pouch Panel

- 1 piece 15" × 1¾" for wrist strap (*optional*)

Lining

- 2 pieces 7¾" × 1¾" for Front/Back Top Panel

- 2 pieces 14¾" × 4⅞" for Small Pouch Panel

Interfacing

- 2 pieces 7¾" × 1¾" for Front/Back Top Panel

- 2 pieces 14¾" × 4⅞" for Small Pouch Panel

Refer to the Small Pouch Panel diagram below to trace and trim the bottom corners of all the Small Pouch Panels using the Gathered Zipper Pouches Corner (Small) pattern (pullout page P1).

```
                    Center

  Dart   Gathered Zipper Pouches   Dart
         Small Pouch Panel

 Trim corner.              Trim corner.
```

Sewing the Front and Back Pieces

1. Fuse the interfacing to the wrong side of the lining pieces.

2. Stitch the darts on the lower corners of the exterior pouch panels. See Sewing Darts (page 17). Press the darts on the front piece toward the center. Press the darts on the back piece toward the outside edge.

3. Make the gathers along the straight top edges of the pouch panels. See Making Gathers (page 17). **FIGURE A**

4. Place and pin a pouch panel and a top panel with right sides together. Sew each set of pieces together and press the seams toward the top panel. **FIGURE B**

5. Topstitch the top panels ⅛″ from the seam. **FIGURE C**

6. Repeat Steps 2–5 for the lining pieces.

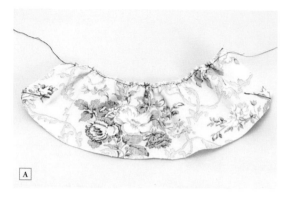

A

B

C

Attaching the Wrist Strap

1. Sew the strap piece. See Strap A (page 18).

2. Fold the strap in half. Place and baste it onto the left side edge of the top panel. **FIGURE D**

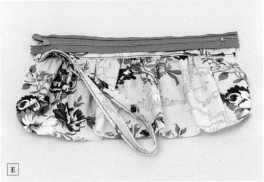

Installing the Zipper

1. Close the zipper and lay it on the exterior top panel with right sides together. You will be able to see the wrong side of the zipper. Pin the zipper and panel in place. Stitch the panel and zipper using a zipper foot, sewing ¼″ from the zipper coil. Backstitch to secure. **FIGURE E**

2. Place the lining piece and exterior with the zipper installed with right sides together. The zipper will now be between the exterior and the lining.

3. Pin and stitch the 3 layers together along the previous stitching line. **FIGURE F**

4. Flip the lining over to the wrong side and press. Topstitch the top panel close to the seam through all the layers.

5. Repeat Steps 1–4 for the other exterior and lining pieces. **FIGURE G**

Assembling the Exterior and Lining

1. Gather each exterior bottom until it is 16″ wide for large, 15″ wide for medium, or 12″ wide for small. **FIGURE H**

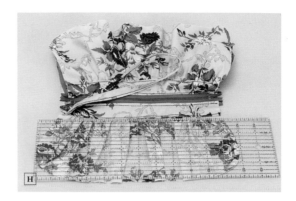

2. Repeat Step 1 for the lining pieces.

3. Match the exteriors with right sides together and then place the lining with right sides together. Open the zipper before you sew all the way around the pouch. It's very difficult to turn it right side out when the zipper is closed. Pin and sew all around the pouch. Carefully sew over the zipper coils. Leave a 4″ gap on the bottom of the lining to turn it right side out. Backstitch at each end. **FIGURE I**

4. Notch the curved seam and clip the zipper panel seams. **FIGURE J**

5. Turn the pouch right side out through the opening in the lining. Using a turning tool, push out the curved corners. Stitch the opening closed. Press the pouch flat.

Gathered Zipper Pouches

Madison Metal Purse and Coin Case

Want to make a handmade present that looks professional? The Madison Metal Purse and Coin Case is the perfect project! Thanks to the metal clasps on the opening of the purse, no coins will ever spill out, no matter how much it's tossed around. It is also a very practical gift. The pleats give extra storage space for keys, change, and cosmetics. Try your hand at working with metal frames in this easy project.

FINISHED SIZES

Purse: 10" wide × 3¾" high × 1½" deep
Coin Case: 6⅛" wide × 4¾" high

SKILL LEVEL Beginner ✿

MATERIALS

Amounts are based on 42"-wide fabric and are for the purse and coin case set.

⅜ yard for exterior

⅜ yard for lining

⅝ yard of fusible interfacing

4¾" × 2½" round metal frame for coin case

8" × 3" rectangle or curved metal frame for purse

Crimping tool

Fabric glue

Paper cord: 1 yard

Leather label (*optional*)

Corsage (*optional*)

NOTE

• A ⅜" seam allowance is included on the pattern.

• Backstitch at the beginning and ends of each seam.

Madison Metal Purse and Coin Case

Draw the pattern directly on the wrong side of a single layer of fabric. Transfer all points and reference marks to the fabric. Cut out the exterior, lining, and interfacing.

Purse
Use the Madison Metal Purse Exterior Front and Back and Lining Front and Back patterns (pullout pages P1 and P2).

Exterior
- 2 Exterior Front and Back pieces

Lining
- 2 Lining Front and Back pieces

Interfacing
- 2 Lining Front and Back pieces

Coin Case
Use the Madison Coin Case Front and Back patterns (pullout page P2).

Exterior
- 2 Front and Back pieces

Lining
- 2 Front and Back pieces

Interfacing
- 2 Front and Back pieces

Sewing the Exterior and Lining

Omit the pleating steps when making the coin purse.

1. Fuse the interfacing onto the wrong side of the lining pieces following the manufacturer's instructions.

2. With the exterior front piece right side up, fold the pleats as indicated on the pattern, aligning the pleat with the placement line, and pin. Repeat for each pleat. **FIGURE A**

3. Pin and sew the exterior front and back pieces with right sides together from a point A around the bottom and to the other point A. **FIGURE B**

4. Clip the corners. **FIGURE C**

5. Repeat Steps 3 and 4 for the lining. Leave an opening for turning. **FIGURE D**

Madison Metal Purse and Coin Case

Assembling the Exterior and Lining

1. Turn the exterior right side out. Insert the exterior into the lining with right sides together. **FIGURE E**

2. Pin the exterior and lining together by their top seams. Sew the front pieces from point A around the top to the second point A. Turn the purse over and sew the back pieces in the same manner. **FIGURE F**

3. Clip the curved seam. **FIGURE G**

4. Turn the purse right side out. Stitch the lining opening closed.

5. Press the top opening. Topstitch ⅛" away from the edge. **FIGURE H**

6. Insert the purse into the metal frame. See Installing a Metal Frame (page 16).

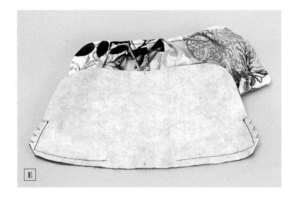

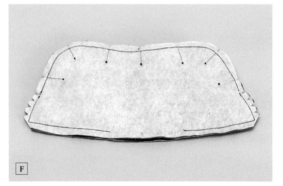

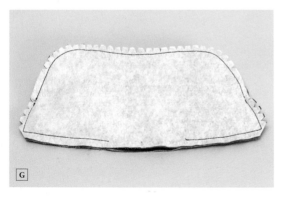

Madison Metal Purse and Coin Case

Jayleen Clutch

This clutch is simple but classy and modern. Make several, changing the fabric to work with simple jeans and a tee, formal wear, or a dress for a special evening. You could also omit the bow for a simpler style.

FINISHED SIZES

Large: 13" wide × 6½" high × 1¾" deep
Small: 6¾" wide × 4¼" high × 1½" deep

SKILL LEVEL Beginner ❀

MATERIALS

Amounts are based on 42"-wide fabric.

Large Clutch

1 yard for exterior (for contrasting bow, ½ yard for bag plus ½ yard for bow)

½ yard for lining

¾ yard of fusible interfacing

7" all-purpose zipper for lining zipper pocket

¾" (18mm) magnetic snap

> **NOTE**
> - A ⅜" seam allowance is included on the pattern.
> - Backstitch at the beginning and end of each seam.

Jayleen Clutch

Large Clutch

Transfer all points and reference marks to the fabric. Cut out the exterior, lining, and interfacing.

Exterior

- 2 pieces 15¼" × 7¾" for Front and Back
- 1 piece 14⅞" × 8¼" for Flap
- 2 pieces 15¼" × 6¼" for Base Bow
- 2 pieces 14" × 7" for Upper Bow
- 2 pieces 4¼" × 8½" for Bow Center

Lining

- 2 pieces 15¼" × 7¾" for Front and Back
- 1 piece 14⅞" × 8¼" for Flap
- 2 pieces 7" × 4½" for Lining Zipper Pockets

Interfacing

- 2 pieces 15¼" × 7¾" for Front and Back
- 1 piece 14⅞" × 8¼" for Flap

Refer to the Large Front and Back diagram below to mark all the front and back pieces. Trace and trim 2 corners using the Jayleen Clutch Large Front and Back Corner pattern (pullout page P1).

Refer to the Large Flap diagram below to mark all the flap pieces. Trace and trim 2 corners using the Jayleen Clutch Large Flap Corner pattern (pullout page P1).

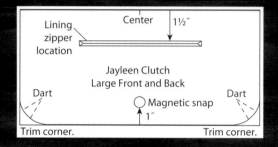

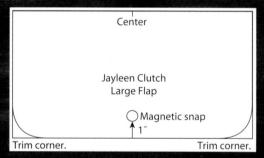

MATERIALS

Amounts are based on 42"-wide fabric.

Small Clutch

¼ yard for exterior

¼ yard for lining

¼ yard of interfacing

½" (12mm) magnetic snap

Leather or woven label (*optional*)

NOTE

- A ⅜" seam allowance is included on the pattern.

- Backstitch at the beginning and end of each seam.

CUTTING

Small Clutch

Draw the pattern directly onto the wrong side of a single layer of fabric. Transfer all points and reference marks to the fabric. Cut out the exterior, lining, and interfacing.

Exterior

- 2 pieces 8¼" × 5½" for Front and Back
- 1 piece 8" × 6" for Flap

Lining

- 2 pieces 8¼" × 5½" for Front and Back
- 1 piece 8" × 6" for Flap

Interfacing

- 2 pieces 8¼" × 5½" for Front and Back
- 1 piece 8" × 6" for Flap

Refer to the Small Front and Back diagram below to mark all the front and back pieces. Trace and trim 2 corners using the Jayleen Clutch Front and Back Corner pattern (pullout page P1).

Refer to the Small Flap diagram below to mark all the flap pieces. Trace and trim 2 corners using the Jayleen Clutch Small Flap Corner pattern (pullout page P1).

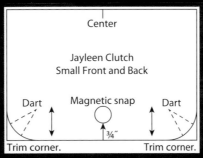

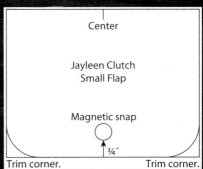

Making the Pockets

1. Fuse the interfacing on the wrong side of the exterior pieces, following the manufacturer's instructions.

2. Make the lining pocket. See Zipper Pocket (page 14). **FIGURE A**

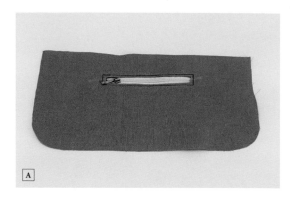

Making the Bow

The bow is on the large clutch only.

1. Pin and sew the front and back pieces of the base bow along the long ends of the fabric with right sides together. Repeat this step for the bow center piece. **FIGURE B**

2. Turn the base bow and bow center pieces right side out through the sides. Press and topstitch ⅛″ away from the seams. **FIGURE C**

3. Pin and sew the front and back upper bow pieces along all the edges, leaving a gap for turning. Trim the corners. **FIGURE D**

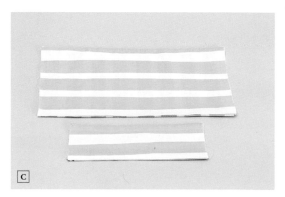

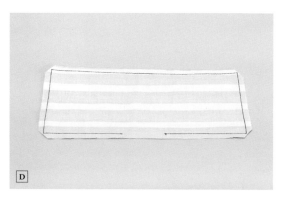

4. Turn the upper bow right side out through the open gap. Press and topstitch all 4 edges, ⅛″ away from the seams, pivoting at the corners. Center the upper bow on the base bow. Stitch through the center of the upper and lower bows with a gathering stitch. Pull and tie the thread on an end so that the fabric scrunches in the middle to a height of 3½″. **FIGURE E**

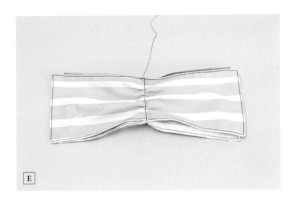

E

5. Fold the center piece in half widthwise and sew the short ends together. Turn it right side out. **FIGURE F**

6. Insert the base and upper bow into the center piece, until the center piece covers the gathering stitches. Hand stitch the center piece to the back side of the base bow to secure them together. **FIGURE G**

F

G

Making the Exterior and Lining

1. Attach the magnetic snap onto the exterior front and the lining flap. See Applying a Magnetic Snap (page 9).

2. Pin and stitch the darts on the exterior front and back pieces. See Sewing Darts (page 17).

3. Pin and sew the exterior front and back pieces with right sides together, making a U shape. **FIGURE H**

4. Clip the curved seam. Turn it right side out. **FIGURE I**

5. Sew the lining as in Steps 2–4, leaving a gap at the bottom for turning.

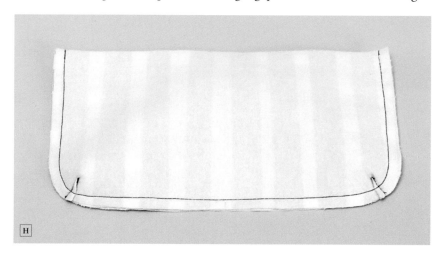

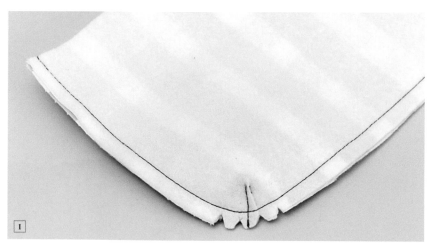

Sewing the Flap

1. Baste the base ends of the assembled bow onto the right and left side ends of the exterior flap piece. Hand stitch the back of the assembled bow center to the flap. **FIGURE J**

2. Place the flap lining and exterior with right sides together. Pin and stitch together, being careful not to catch the upper bow in the seam. Leave the top open. **FIGURE K**

3. Clip the curved seam and turn it right side out. Press the flap and topstitch ¼″ away from the edge.

4. Fold the upper bow ends to the center, away from the side seams. **FIGURE L**

5. Position the flap onto the back of the bag exterior with exterior sides together, matching the center marks. Then pin and baste the flap to the bag. **FIGURE M**

J

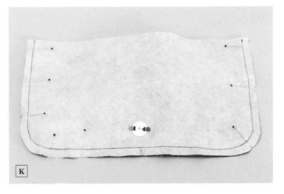

K

L

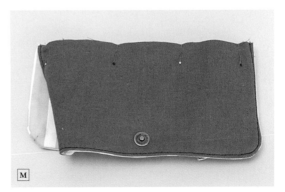

M

Assembling the Exterior and Lining

1. Press the exterior and lining side seams open. Place the exterior into the lining with the right sides together, sandwiching the flap between the 2 pieces. **FIGURE N**

2. Match the side seams. Pin the exterior and lining together; sew around the top opening of the bag. **FIGURE O**

3. Trim the corner seams at the top of the seams. **FIGURE P**

4. Turn the bag right side out through the opening, then stitch the opening closed.

5. Tuck the lining into the exterior. Press the top edge of the clutch and topstitch ⅛" away from the edge and the flap seam. **FIGURE Q**

Jayleen Clutch

Evelyn Clutch

This clutch is a real eye-catcher. The key is to properly match
or coordinate the piping with the main clutch fabric. The side
darts are easy and make the clutch roomy.

FINISHED SIZE 11½″ wide × 5¾″ high × 1½″ deep

SKILL LEVEL Confident Beginner ❀ ❀

MATERIALS

Amounts are based on 42″-wide fabric.

⅜ yard for exterior

½ yard coordinating fabric for exterior flap piping and tab (*tab is optional*)

½ yard for lining

¾ yard of fusible interfacing

¾″ (18mm) magnetic snap

7″ all-purpose zipper for lining pocket

Buckle with 2″ opening (for tab) or twist lock

¾ yard ⅛″ cording for piping

> NOTE
> • A ⅜″ seam allowance is included on the pattern.
>
> • Backstitch at the beginning and end of each seam.

Evelyn Clutch

Use the Evelyn Clutch Front and Back and Flap patterns (pullout page P2).

Draw the pattern directly onto the wrong side of a single layer of fabric. Transfer all points and reference marks to the fabric. Cut out the exterior, lining, and interfacing.

Exterior

- 2 Front and Back pieces
- 1 Flap piece

Exterior Coordinating Fabric

- 2 pieces 3¼″ × 7¾″ for tab (*optional, not shown*)
- 1 bias strip 1½″ × 24″ for piping

Lining

- 2 Front and Back pieces
- 1 Flap piece
- 2 pieces 7″ × 4″ for Zipper Pocket

Interfacing

- 2 Front and Back pieces
- 1 Flap piece

Making the Exterior and Lining

1. Fuse the interfacing to the wrong side of the exterior front and back pieces, following the manufacturer's instructions.

2. Attach half of the magnetic snap onto the exterior front. See Applying a Magnetic Snap (page 9).

3. Sew the darts. See Sewing Darts (page 17).

4. Place the exterior front and back pieces with right sides together. The front and back darts should be facing opposite directions.

5. Pin and sew the exterior using a ⅜″ seam allowance, making a U shape and back-stitching on both ends. **FIGURE A**

6. Clip the curved seams. Turn it right side out. **FIGURE B**

7. Sew the lining zipper pocket. See Zipper Pocket (page 14).

8. Repeat Steps 3–6 for the lining; leave a 4″ gap for turning.

Making the Piping

1. Center the ⅛″ cording down the center of the bias strip.

2. Fold the strip in half, over the cording.

3. Stitch together ¼″ from the raw edge, being careful not to stretch the bias edges.

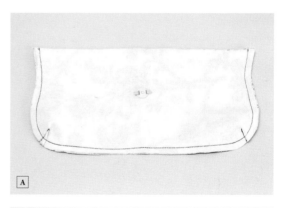

Stitching the Flap

1. Place the flap tab pieces with right sides together. Pin, leaving the top open for turning. Stitch and trim the corners. **FIGURE C**

2. Turn the tab right side out. Press the tab and topstitch ¼″ away from the edge. **FIGURE D**

3. Place the piping and flap with right sides together. Pin the center and each end first.

4. Pin the rest, clipping the piping seam allowance, if needed. Stitch the piping to the flap with a ¼″ seam. **FIGURE E**

5. Fuse the interfacing to the wrong side of the lining piece, following the manufacturer's instructions. Attach the second half of the magnetic snap onto the flap lining. See Applying a Magnetic Snap (page 9).

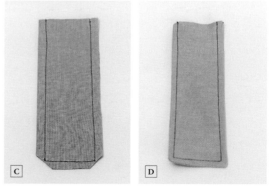

6. Place the exterior flap and lining flap pieces with right sides together. Pin in place and stitch only the curved seam with a ⅜″ seam, leaving the straight edge unstitched. **FIGURE F**

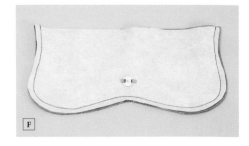

7. Clip the curved seams. **FIGURE G**

8. Turn it right side out. Press the flap and topstitch ⅛″ away from the piping seam.

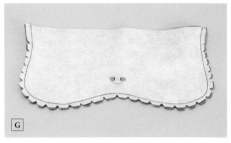

9. Center the tab on the flap and baste. **FIGURE H**

10. Center the flap onto the back piece of the case with exterior sides together, aligning the raw edges. Pin and baste in place. **FIGURE I**

Assembling the Exterior and Lining

1. Insert the exterior into the lining, right sides together. The flap and tab should be sandwiched between the lining and exterior. **FIGURE J**

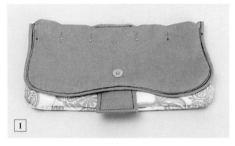

2. Pin the exterior and lining together around the opening of the bag.

3. Stitch around the opening of the bag. Trim the corners at the top of the seams.

4. Turn the bag right side out through the opening in the lining. Stitch the opening closed. Tuck the lining into the exterior. Press the top opening of the bag. Topstitch around the opening ⅛″ from the edge.

5. Slide the buckle onto the tab.

6. Hand stitch the back of the tab to the flap.

Evelyn Clutch

Julianna Bag

The round shape and design of this bag make it a sophisticated piece that anyone can sew. The handle can be made any length you choose. As a shoulder bag, it is the perfect size to tuck under your arm. The darts in the front and back allow for plenty of space to carry a lot of items.

FINISHED SIZE 11¾" wide × 7⅛" high × 2¾" deep

SKILL LEVEL Beginner ❀

MATERIALS

Amounts are based on 42"-wide fabric.

½ yard for exterior

⅞ yard for lining

¾ yard of fusible interfacing

18mm magnetic snap

½" buckle or ½" O-ring

Purchased or handmade flowers (*optional embellishment*)

> NOTE
> • Seam allowances are ⅜" unless otherwise specified.
> • Backstitch at the beginning and end of each seam.

Use the Julianna Bag Front and Back and Flap patterns (pullout page P2).

Draw the patterns directly onto the wrong side of a single layer of fabric. Transfer all points and reference marks to the fabric. Cut out the exterior, lining, and interfacing.

Exterior

- 2 Front and Back pieces
- 1 Flap piece
- 1 piece 19″ × 2¼″ for Strap
- 1 piece 5″ × 2¼″ for Loop

Lining

- 2 Front and Back pieces
- 1 Flap piece

Interfacing

- 2 Front and Back pieces
- 1 Flap piece

Making the Exterior and Lining

1. Fuse the interfacing to the wrong side of the exterior front and back, following the manufacturer's instructions.

2. Attach half of the magnetic snap onto the exterior front and lining flap. See Applying a Magnetic Snap (page 9).

3. Sew the darts. See Sewing Darts (page 17). **FIGURE A**

4. Place the exterior front and back pieces with right sides together. The back piece darts will face the opposite direction as the front piece darts. Pin and sew the exterior, making a U shape and backstitching on both ends. Clip the curved corner seams. Turn it right side out. **FIGURE B**

5. Sew the lining in the same manner, leaving a 5″ gap for turning. **FIGURE C**

Constructing the Flap

1. Fuse the interfacing to the wrong side of the lining piece, following the manufacturer's instructions. Attach the second half of the magnetic snap onto the lining flap. See Applying a Magnetic Snap (page 9).

2. Place the exterior flap and lining flap pieces with right sides together. Pin in place and stitch only the lower curved seam, leaving the upper edge unstitched. Clip the curved seam. **FIGURE D**

3. Turn it right side out. Press the flap and topstitch ½" away from the edge. **FIGURE E**

4. Center the flap onto the back piece of the case with exterior sides together, aligning the raw edges. Pin and baste in place. **FIGURE F**

A

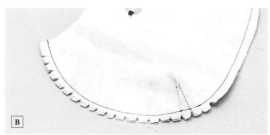

B

C

D

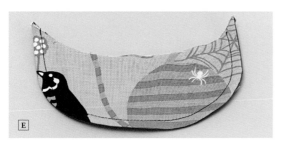

E

F

Stitching the Loop and Strap

1. Make the loop piece. See Strap A (page 18). Insert the loop into the O-ring or buckle.

2. Make the strap piece. See Strap B (page 19).

3. Baste the loop and strap onto the bag, matching the ends to the center of the side seams. **FIGURE H**

Assembling the Exterior and Lining

1. Press the exterior and lining seams open. Place the exterior into the lining with right sides together, sandwiching the flap and strap pieces between the 2 pieces. Pin the exterior and lining together. **FIGURE I**

2. Sew around the top opening of the bag. **FIGURE J**

3. Clip the curved seam and trim the corner seams. Turn the bag right side out through the opening and stitch the opening closed. Tuck the lining into the exterior. Press the top opening of the clutch and topstitch ⅛″ away from the top. Insert the strap into the buckle or O-ring and sew the strap at the desired location. **FIGURE K**

Julianna Bag

Linnea Ruffled Bag

Introducing a cute, petite ruffled purse, the Linnea Ruffled Bag! With a simple process to attach the zipper, the pattern is a very suitable project for newer sewists. The ruffles can be omitted and you will still have an adorable bag for the quick outings where you need only your wallet and phone. Want to carry it around in your purse instead? Skip the handle and you can make this into a small pouch companion!

FINISHED SIZE 11″ wide × 5⅞″ high

SKILL LEVEL Confident Beginner ❀ ❀

MATERIALS

Amounts are based on 42″-wide fabric.

½ yard for exterior

¼ yard for lining

⅜ yard of fusible interfacing

10″ all-purpose zipper

7″ all-purpose zipper for lining zipper pocket

½″ O-ring for strap

Leather label (*optional*)

NOTE

• A ⅜″ seam allowance is included on the pattern.

• Backstitch at the beginning and end of each seam.

Linnea Ruffled Bag

Use the Linnea Ruffled Bag Front and Back pattern (pullout page P2).

Transfer all points and reference marks to the fabric. Cut out the exterior, lining, and interfacing.

Exterior

- 1 piece 2¼″ × 6¾″ for Exterior Center Panel

- 2 Exterior Front and Back pieces For the ruffled version, cut the front piece in half along the Front Ruffle cutting line.

- 2 pieces 3¾″ × 10″ for Center Ruffle Panels

- 4 pieces 4″ × 10″ for Side Ruffle Panels

- 1 piece 4″ × 2″ for loop

- 1 piece 42″ × 2″ for strap

Lining

- 2 Front and Back pieces

- 2 pieces 7″ × 4″ for Zipper Pocket

Interfacing

- 2 Front and Back pieces

Making the Ruffle

1. Fold each ruffle panel in half lengthwise with wrong sides together. Gather the ruffle pieces. See Making Gathers (page 17). **FIGURE A**

2. Place a side ruffle panel onto the front half piece with right sides together and the raw edge of the ruffle 2¾″ from the center raw edge. Pin the ends first, adjust the gathers to fit, and then pin the rest of the ruffle. Sew the ruffle to the front using a ⅜″ seam allowance. **FIGURE B**

3. Repeat Step 2 to attach the next side ruffle over the first, with the raw edge of the ruffle 1⅜″ from the center edge.

4. Repeat Step 2 to attach the center ruffle, matching the raw edges.

5. Repeat Steps 2–4 to attach the ruffles to the other front half piece. **FIGURE C**

6. Sew the exterior center panel and exterior side panel with right sides together. Press the seam toward the center. Topstitch ⅛″ away from the edge. **FIGURE D**

7. Attach the other side in the same manner. **FIGURE E**

Installing the Zipper and Lining

1. Fuse the interfacing to the wrong side of the lining pieces, following the manufacturer's instructions.

2. Install the lining zipper pocket. See Zipper Pocket (page 14).

3. Sew the exterior and lining darts. See Sewing Darts (page 17).

4. Close the zipper and lay it on the exterior front panel with right sides together. You will be able to see the wrong side of the zipper. Pin in place and, using a zipper foot, stitch the zipper to the top panel ⅛″ from the edge of the tape. Backstitch to secure. **FIGURE F**

5. Place the lining piece and zippered exterior with right sides together. The zipper will now be between the exterior and the lining. Stitch, leaving ⅜″ unsewn on both ends. **FIGURE G**

6. Flip the lining over to the wrong side and press. Topstitch the top panel close to the zipper coils through all the layers, leaving ⅜″ unsewn on both ends. **FIGURE H**

7. Repeat Steps 4–6 for the other exterior and lining pieces.

A

B

C

D

E

F

G

H

Stitching the Loop and Strap

1. Make the loop piece. See Strap A (page 18). Insert the loop piece into the ring. **FIGURE I**

2. Fold the loop piece in half with wrong sides together. Place the loop piece onto the zipper end and baste.

3. Sew the strap. See Strap B (page 19).

4. Place the strap onto the other side zipper end and baste. **FIGURE J**

Assembling the Exterior and Lining

1. Match the exterior front and back pieces with right sides together. Pin and stitch from point A on a corner to point A on the other corner. **FIGURE K**

2. Sew the lining in the same manner, leaving a 4″ opening for turning. **FIGURE L**

3. Clip the exterior and lining round corner seams.

4. Fold the top corners in, right sides together, over the loop and with the zipper coils meeting in the center.

5. Stitch across the seam, sewing back and forth several times to reinforce. **FIGURE M**

6. Turn the bag right side out. Press the bag and stitch the lining opening closed.

7. Insert the finished end of the long strap through the O-ring. Pull the strap to the desired length. Pin and stitch the end of the strap ⅛″ from the edge. **FIGURE N**

Linnea Ruffled Bag

Genevieve Ruffled Bag

The ruffles on the center of the bag give an extra sense of volume

to the bag, like its own personal trait. The addition of a zipper and

elastic pockets inside allow for easy practical use and convenience.

The Genevieve Ruffled Bag is more suited for intermediate sewers.

Beginners can omit the ruffles if they wish.

FINISHED SIZE 14" wide × 9¼" high × 3¼" deep

SKILL LEVEL Intermediate ❀ ❀ ❀

MATERIALS

Amounts are based on 42"-wide fabric.

1½ yards for exterior

⅞ yard solid color for double ruffle
(*optional, not shown*)

1 yard for lining

1 yard of fusible interfacing

14" all-purpose zipper

7" all-purpose zipper for lining

½ yard of ½"-wide elastic

1" ring for loop

3 yards of double-fold bias tape for inside binding

tip If the zipper is too long, shorten
it by whipstitching several times at
the correct length, and then cut it 1"
below the whip-stitched point.

> **NOTE**
> - A ⅜" seam allowance is included
>   on the pattern.
> - Backstitch at the beginning and
>   end of each seam.

Genevieve Ruffled Bag

CUTTING

Use the Genevieve Ruffled Bag Front Side, Front Center, Back, Gusset, and Elastic Pocket patterns (pullout pages P1 and P2).

Draw the pattern directly onto the wrong side of a single layer of fabric. Transfer all points and reference marks to the fabric. Cut out the exterior, lining, and interfacing.

Exterior

- 2 Front Side pieces
- 1 Front Center piece
- 1 Back piece
- 1 Gusset piece
- 2 pieces 13¼" × 1⅛" for Zipper Panel
- 1 piece 17½" × 4¾" for top Ruffle
- 5 pieces 42" × 4" for remaining Ruffles
- 1 piece 17½" × 4" for loop
- 1 piece 24" × 4" for strap

Lining

- 2 Front and Back pieces
- 1 Gusset piece
- 2 pieces 13¼" × 1⅛" for Zipper Panel
- 1 Elastic Pocket piece
- 1 piece 7" × 6" for Zipper Pocket

Interfacing

- 2 Back pieces
- 1 Gusset piece
- 2 pieces 13¼" × 1⅛" for Zipper Panel

Double ruffle (optional)

- 6 pieces 44" × 4"

Assembling the Front

1. Set aside the top ruffle piece. Sew all the remaining ruffle pieces together end-to-end and press the seams open. Fold the ruffle piece in half lengthwise, with wrong sides together, and press. Cut 3 pieces 37" long, and 1 each at 35", 33", and 31" long.

2. Gather each ruffle to the length shown.

   FIGURE A

   Ruffle #1 (bottom):   37" gathered to 15¾"

   Ruffle #2:   37" gathered to 14¾"

   Ruffle #3:   37" gathered to 13¾"

   Ruffle #4:   35" gathered to 12¼"

   Ruffle #5:   33" gathered to 10¾"

   Ruffle #6:   31" gathered to 9¾"

   Ruffle #7 (top):   17½" gathered to 7¾"

3. Draw the ruffle placement lines as indicated on the pattern on the front center piece, using a washable pen or chalk. Place ruffle #1 onto the front bottom piece with right sides together and the edge of the ruffle along the line. Adjust the gathers so they are

even. Pin the ends first; then pin the center and sew together with a ⅜″ seam. **FIGURE B**

4. Attach the remaining ruffles in the same manner. Match the raw edge of the top ruffle with the raw edge of the center panel. **FIGURES C & D**

Double Ruffle (*optional*): Prepare a second set of ruffles following Step 1 (page 64). Attach the second ruffle piece ¼″ above the first ruffle, and continue as in Step 2. Trim the last solid ruffle ¼″ so that it is shorter than the print ruffle.

A

B

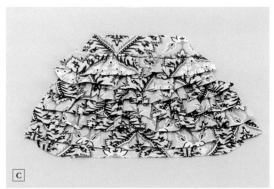

C

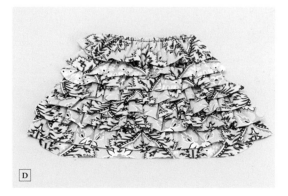

D

5. Place each side piece onto the center panel with right sides together. Pin and sew the pieces together. **FIGURE E**

6. Press the seam toward the side piece and topstitch ⅛″ away from the seams. **FIGURE F**

7. Place the zipper panel onto the front piece. Pin and sew together, stopping ⅜″ from each end. Backstitch on both ends. Attach the back piece and the zipper panel in the same manner. **FIGURE G**

Sewing the Lining

1. Fuse the interfacing to the wrong side of the lining pieces, following the manufacturer's instructions.

2. Sew the elastic pocket to the lining. See Elastic Pocket (page 13).

3. Sew the zipper pocket to the lining. See Zipper Pocket (page 14). **FIGURE H**

4. Repeat Assembling the Front, Step 7 (above) and attach the zipper panels to the lining pieces.

E

F

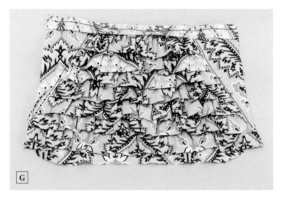

G

H

Installing the Zipper

Attach the zipper. See Gathered Zipper
Pouches, Installing the Zipper (page 25).
FIGURE I

Making the Strap and Loop Pieces

1. Stitch the loop piece. See Strap A
   (page 18). Insert the loop piece into
   the ring. Fold the loop in half and
   baste the ends together. **FIGURE J**

2. Stitch the strap piece. See Strap B
   (page 19).

Assembling the Bag

1. Place the exterior gusset and lining
   gusset with wrong sides together. Baste
   the exterior and lining gusset along the
   long edges. Baste the exterior and lining
   front and back pieces along the sides
   and bottom. **FIGURE K**

2. Match the upper edges and pin the
   gusset piece to the front piece with right
   sides together. Pin and sew the bag
   using a ⅜″ seam allowance, starting ⅜″
   from the top edge, continuing around
   the bottom to the other side, and
   stopping ⅜″ from the end. Backstitch
   on both ends. Repeat this process for
   the back piece. **FIGURE L**

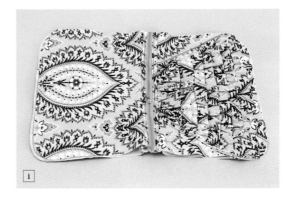

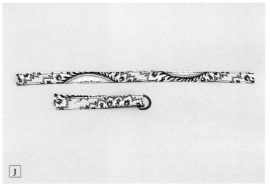

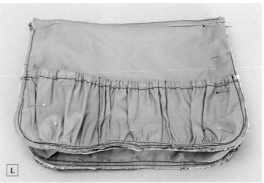

Genevieve Ruffled Bag

3. Insert the loop piece between the gusset and the zipper panel, folding the zipper panel back to the gusset, with right sides together, and pin. Insert the strap between the gusset and the zipper panel on the opposite side and pin. Sew the zipper panel to the gusset piece on each side. **FIGURE M**

4. Unfold 1 side of the bias binding, fold the short end in ½″, and press. Place the raw edge of the bias binding at the beginning edge of the front side inner seam with right sides together. Pin in place and stitch along the front and back seams, overlapping the beginning ½″. **FIGURES N & O**

5. Fold the bias tape over and encase the seam. Topstitch on the bias tape following the first sewing line. **FIGURE P**

6. Insert the strap into the ring and fold the strap, adjusting to the desired length. Stitch several times over the strap for strength.

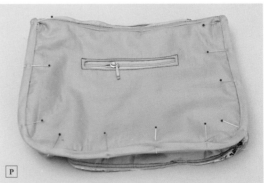

Genevieve Ruffled Bag

Thelma Bag

Characterized by its beautiful gathers, the Thelma Bag is a zippered bag with a unique front. The front is composed of gathers and darts, which allow for extra storage room inside. Because of the numerous curved edges, the bias binding, and the zippers, the project is recommended for confident beginners.

FINISHED SIZE 21½″ wide × 13¼″ high

SKILL LEVEL Confident Beginner ❄ ❄

MATERIALS

Amounts are based on 42″-wide fabric.

1⅞ yards for exterior

2 yards for lining

2 yards of fusible interfacing

23″ all-purpose zipper

8″ all-purpose zipper for lining pockets

2″ buckle or D-ring

> **NOTE**
> - A ⅜″ seam allowance is included on the pattern.
> - Backstitch at the beginning and end of each seam.

Thelma Bag

Use the Thelma Bag Front Bottom, Front Top, and Back patterns (pullout pages P1 and P2).

Draw the pattern directly onto the wrong side of a folded layer of fabric. Transfer all points and reference marks to the wrong side of each piece. Cut out the exterior, lining, and interfacing.

Exterior

- 1 Front Top piece
- 1 Front Bottom piece
- 1 Back piece
- 1 piece 8″ × 8¼″ for Loop
- 1 piece 8″ × 14″ for Strap

Lining

- 2 Back pieces
- 2 pieces 7″ × 6″ for Zipper Pocket
- 2 pieces 8″ × 6″ for Pocket
- 1 bias strip 1¾″ × 55″ for lining bias binding
- 2 bias strips 1¾″ × 4″ for lining bias binding on strap seams

Interfacing

- 2 Back pieces
  (If interfacing is only 20″ wide, you will need to fuse more than 1 piece to make a larger piece.)

Sewing the Exterior

1. Fuse the interfacing to the wrong side of the lining pieces per the manufacturer's instructions.

2. Sew the exterior darts. See Sewing Darts (page 17). **FIGURE A**

3. Make the gathers on the top edge of the exterior front bottom piece as indicated on the pattern. See Making Gathers (page 17). **FIGURE B**

4. Place the front bottom piece and front top piece with right sides together. Pin the centers first and then match the ends.

5. Pin the rest and stitch together. Clip the top seam, if needed. **FIGURE C**

6. Press the seam toward the top piece and topstitch ⅛″ away from the edge. **FIGURE D**

7. Sew the lining pocket 3½″ down from the top. See Standard Pocket (page 12).

8. Sew the lining zipper pocket 3″ down from the top. See Zipper Pocket (page 14). **FIGURE E**

Installing the Zipper

Install the zipper along the inner curve of the front top piece and the back. See Gathered Zipper Pouches, Installing the Zipper (page 25). **FIGURE F**

Stitching the Strap and Loop

1. Make the loop piece. See Strap A (page 18). Insert the loop piece into the ring.

2. Fold the loop piece in half with wrong sides together. Place the loop piece onto the zipper end and baste. **FIGURE G**

3. Sew the strap. See Strap B (page 19).

4. Place the strap onto the other end of the zipper and baste. **FIGURE H**

Assembling the Exterior and Lining

1. Baste the exterior front and the lining front pieces together around the outside edge. Repeat for the back. Pin the front and back together, with exterior sides facing each other. Stitch around the outside edge through all layers. **FIGURE I**

2. Prepare the bias binding by folding each strip in half lengthwise and press. Unfold and then fold the raw edges in to the center crease. Fold along the center crease and press again.

A

B

C

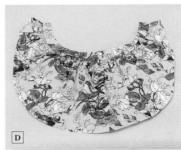

D

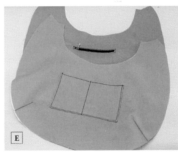

E

F

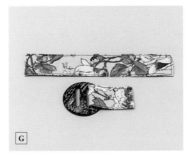

G

H

I

3. Unfold the long length of bias binding. Beginning at the outside corner of 1 side of the bag, pin the raw edge of the bias binding to the outside edge of the bag, with right sides together. Pin all the way around to the outside corner on the other side.

4. Stitch along the crease line of the binding closest to the outside edge. Fold the binding over to encase the raw edge and pin.

5. Topstitch the binding ⅛″ from the inner fold of the binding, through all layers. Trim any excess binding even with the outside corner. **FIGURE J**

6. With the bag still inside out and the zipper open, center the unfinished end of the strap over the side seam and pin, with right sides together and folding the lining binding to a side. Fold the zipper panels over to cover the strap, with the zipper coils meeting in the center.

7. Stitch across the seam, sewing back and forth several times to reinforce.

8. Unfold a 4″ piece of bias binding. Center the binding over the trimmed seam and pin the raw edge of the bias binding in place, with right sides together. Stitch along the crease line closest to the edge of the trimmed seam. **FIGURE K**

9. Fold in the ends of the binding, even with the ends of the seam. **FIGURE L**

10. Fold the binding over to encase the raw edge and pin. **FIGURE M**

11. Topstitch the binding ⅛″ from the inner fold of the binding, through all layers. Repeat for the loop piece, making sure it is facing the right way.

12. Turn the bag right side out. Insert the remaining end of the strap into the buckle, taking care not to twist the strap and adjusting the length as necessary, and stitch. **FIGURE N**

Thelma Bag

Susan Boston Bag

The Susan Boston Bag has the stable, standard shape of a Boston bag,

but with the addition of pockets on the front for more convenience.

It also includes elastic pockets on the interior for organization. It is

highly customizable and works with many different styles of fabric.

You can personalize it further by including straps and using it as a

backpack instead! Due to the process of adding the gusset, the project

is recommended for at least intermediate sewers.

FINISHED SIZE 15" wide × 14¾" high × 5¼" deep

SKILL LEVEL Intermediate ✿ ✿ ✿

MATERIALS

Amounts are based on 42"-wide fabric.

1 yard for exterior

⅜ yard for front pocket

2 yards for lining

2 yards of fusible interfacing

22" all-purpose zipper

15" all-purpose zipper for front pocket

7" all-purpose zipper for lining pocket

1 yard of ¼"-wide elastic

1 set of 18" leather and webbing handles

3½ yards of piping

> **NOTE**
> - A ⅜" seam allowance is included on the pattern.
>
> - Backstitch at the beginning and end of each seam.

Susan Boston Bag

CUTTING

Transfer all points and reference marks to the fabric. Cut out the exterior, lining, and interfacing.

Bag

Exterior

- 2 pieces 16″ × 15½″ for Front and Back
- 2 pieces 3″ × 21¼″ for Zipper Panel
- 1 piece 5¾″ × 35″ for Gusset

Lining

- 2 pieces 16″ × 15½″ for Front and Back
- 2 pieces 3″ × 21¼″ for Zipper Panel
- 1 piece 5¾″ × 35″ for Gusset
- 2 pieces 7″ × 6″ for Zipper Pocket
- 2 pieces 20″ × 8″ Elastic Pocket
- 2 bias pieces 1¾″ × 6″ for Side Zipper Gusset seams
- 2 bias pieces 1¾″ × 57″ for Front and Back seams (Piece as needed.)

Interfacing

- 2 pieces 16″ × 15½″ for Front and Back
- 2 pieces 3″ × 21¼″ for Zipper Panel
- 1 piece 5¾″ × 35″ for Gusset

Refer to the Front and Back and Lining Elastic Pocket diagrams below to trace and trim the exterior, lining, and interfacing corners using the Susan Boston Bag Front and Back Top and Bottom Corner patterns (pullout page P1).

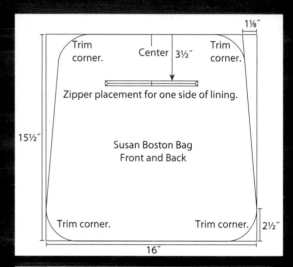

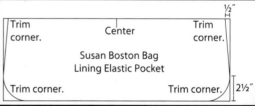

Front Pocket

Exterior

- 1 piece 11″ × 10″ for Front Pocket

- 1 piece 14¼″ × 1½″ for Front Pocket
  Zipper Panel

- 1 piece 23″ × 2″ for Front Pocket Gusset

*Refer to the Front Pocket diagram below
to trace and trim the exterior corners using
the Susan Boston Bag Front Pocket Top and
Bottom Corner patterns (pullout page P1).*

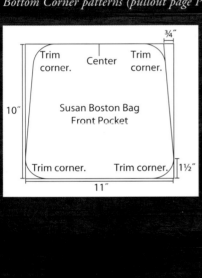

Assembling the Front Pocket

1. Place the front pocket zipper panel onto
the zipper with right sides together.

2. Pin and stitch; press the seam toward
the zipper panel. Topstitch ⅛″ away from
the seam.

3. Place the zipper panel and gusset with right
sides together at each end. Pin in place and
stitch together. Press the seam toward the
gusset and topstitch ⅛″ away from the seam.
Connect the other side in the same manner.

4. Attach the assembled the zipper panel onto the front pocket with right sides together. Match the centers to the front centers. Pin all around the zipper panel. Clip the zipper panel only as necessary to help ease it around the curve of the front piece. Sew around the pocket. Overlock the seam with a serger or zigzag stitch. **FIGURE A**

5. Fold the top edge under ⅜″ to the wrong side and press. Fold it over another ⅜″ and press. **FIGURE B**

6. Place the front pocket centered onto the bag front piece. Pin in place and topstitch around the pocket sides. **FIGURE C**

7. Pin the piping around the edges of the front and back pieces and stitch. See Attaching Piping (page 15). **FIGURE D**

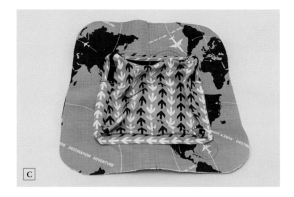

Making the Lining Pocket

1. Fuse the interfacing to the wrong side of the lining front and back, the zipper panels, and the gusset, following the manufacturer's instructions.

2. Make the lining zipper pocket. See Zipper Pocket (page 14).

3. Stitch the elastic pockets, using 14″ elastic pieces for each. See Elastic Pocket (page 13). **FIGURE E**

Connecting the Zipper Panels and Bottom Panel

1. Install the zipper. See Gathered Zipper Pouches, Installing the Zipper (page 25). **FIGURE F**

2. Pin the exterior gusset piece to the lining gusset piece, wrong sides together, and baste. Pin the ends of the assembled zipper panel to the ends of the gusset piece to form a ring, exterior sides together. Stitch the seams. Trim as needed. **FIGURE G**

3. Press the bias pieces in half lengthwise; then open and fold each edge to the center and press again. Pin a 6″ piece of bias binding to the trimmed seam, matching raw edges and with right sides together.

4. Stitch along the crease line closest to the edge of the trimmed seam, backstitching at both ends. Fold the binding over to encase the raw edge and pin.

5. Topstitch the binding ⅛″ from the inner fold of the binding, through all the layers. **FIGURE H**

6. Repeat Steps 2–5 for the seam at the other end.

E

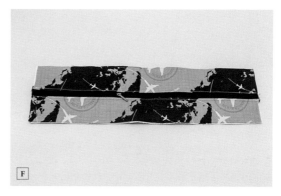

F

G

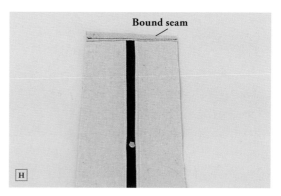

Bound seam

H

Assembling the Bag

1. Fold the zipper/gusset piece to find and mark the centers of the zipper panel and the gusset piece. Pin the zipper/gusset piece to the front, exterior sides together, matching the zipper/gusset piece centers to the front centers and the zipper/gusset piece seams to the seam markings on the front. Clip the zipper/gusset piece only as necessary to help ease it around the curve of the front piece.

2. Stitch the seam, working carefully around the corners.
   FIGURE I

3. Repeat Steps 1 and 2 to attach the back piece. **FIGURE J**

Adding Bias Binding

1. Unfold the 57″ length of bias binding. Fold and press a short end of the bias binding under ⅜″. Beginning at the bottom center of the bag front, pin the raw edge of the bias binding to the outside edge of the bag, with right sides together. Pin all the way around, lapping the end of the bias binding over the folded end ⅜″. **FIGURE K**

2. Stitch along the crease line closest to the outside edge. Fold the binding over to encase the raw edge and pin.

3. Topstitch the binding ⅛″ from the inner fold of the binding, through all layers. Turn the bag right side out and press.

4. Repeat Steps 1–3 to bind the seam on the back piece.

Attaching the Handle

Attach the leather and webbing handles following the manufacturer's instructions, placing the inner edges 2″ from the center.

Susan Boston Bag

Violet Bag

The Violet Bag includes a flap instead of a zipper for easy sewing.
Designed to fit perfectly on your shoulder, the Violet Bag was made
with comfort in mind. This bag has straps attached with rings. Inside
are pockets on both sides—zippered and standard—to allow for secure
storage of important items such as keys and phones.

FINISHED SIZE 16″ wide × 9″ high × 6″ deep

SKILL LEVEL Beginner ❄

MATERIALS

Amounts are based on 42″-wide fabric.

1 yard for exterior

1 yard for lining

1⅝ yards of fusible interfacing

¾″ (18mm) magnetic snap

7″ all-purpose zipper

2″ O- or D-rings, or rectangular
rings, 2″ inside diameter

NOTE

- A ⅜″ seam allowance is
  included on the pattern.

- Backstitch at the beginning
  and end of each seam.

Draw the pattern directly onto the wrong side of a single layer of fabric. Transfer all points and reference marks to the fabric. Cut out the exterior, lining, and interfacing.

Use the Violet Bag Front and Back and Flap patterns (pullout page P2).

Exterior

- 2 Front and Back pieces
- 1 Flap piece
- 1 piece 8″ × 17″ for strap

Lining

- 2 Front and Back pieces
- 1 Flap piece
- 2 pieces 7″ × 6″ for Lining Zipper Pocket
- 2 pieces 11″ × 6¼″ for Lining Standard Pocket

Interfacing

- 2 Front and Back pieces
- 1 Flap piece

Sewing the Exterior

1. Fuse interfacing to the back of the exterior front and back, following the manufacturer's instructions.

2. Attach half of the magnetic snap onto the exterior front. See Applying a Magnetic Snap (page 9).

3. Sew the darts. See Sewing Darts (page 17).

4. Place the exterior front and back pieces with right sides together. The front and back darts should be facing opposite directions.

5. Pin and sew the exterior, making a U shape, using a ⅜″ seam allowance, and back-stitching on both ends. **FIGURE A**

6. Clip the curved corner seams. **FIGURE B**

Making the Lining

1. Make and attach a zipper pocket 2″ below the top edge of 1 lining piece. See Zipper Pocket (page 14). **FIGURE C**

2. Make and attach the standard pocket 2¼″ below the top edge of the other lining piece. See Standard Pocket (page 12).

3. Sew the lining, following Steps 3–5 for Sewing the Exterior, above. Leave a 6″ gap for turning. **FIGURE D**

Stitching the Flap

1. Fuse the interfacing to the wrong side of the lining flap, following the manufacturer's instructions. Attach the second half of the magnetic snap onto the lining flap. See Applying a Magnetic Snap (page 9).

2. Place the exterior flap and lining flap piece with right sides together. Pin in place and stitch only the curved seam, leaving the straight edge unstitched. **FIGURE E**

3. Clip the curved seam and turn it right side out. Press the flap and topstitch ¼" away from the edge. **FIGURE F**

4. Center the flap onto the back piece of the case with exterior sides together, aligning the raw edges. Pin and baste in place. **FIGURE G**

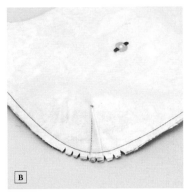
A

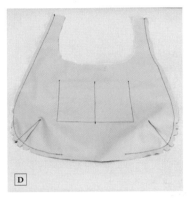
B

C

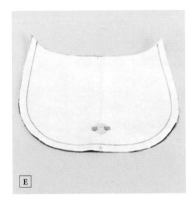
D

E

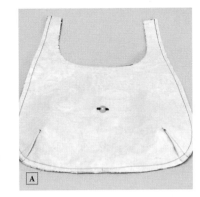
F

G

Assembling the Exterior and Lining

1. Insert the exterior into the lining, right sides together. The flap should be sandwiched between the lining and the exterior. **FIGURE H**

2. Pin and stitch the exterior and the lining together around the opening of the bag. **FIGURE I**

3. Trim the corners at the top of the seams and clip the curved seam. **FIGURE J**

4. Turn the bag right side out through the opening in the lining. Stitch the lining opening closed.

5. Tuck the lining into the exterior. Press the top opening of the bag. Topstitch around the opening ⅛″ from the edge. **FIGURE K**

Finishing the Bag

1. Fold the short ends of the strap in ⅜″ and press. **FIGURE L**

2. Sew the strap. See Strap B (page 19). **FIGURE M**

3. To attach the strap, slip a bag handle extension at the side of the bag through the handle ring. Fold the extension over 1″ toward the lining and stitch in place ⅛″ from the edge of the extension. Attach the other O-ring in the same manner.

4. Insert the strap into the O-ring and pull the strap to your desired length. Pin in place and stitch. Repeat this step for other side. **FIGURE N**

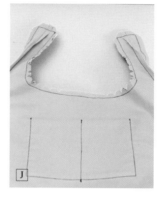

Violet Bag

Valentina Bag

This bag follows the practical style of big, modern bags. It is enormous by design and has the capacity to hold many items of various sizes: laptops, textbooks, groceries, diapers, you name it! It is also an ideal day-trip or beach bag. Using heavier fabrics for this bag will result in a sturdier bag, which will then create a more comfortable option for carrying around heavy items. The short handles are well suited to its size and will equally distribute the weight and resulting stress on the wearer's shoulders or hands.

FINISHED SIZE 17½" wide × 13½" high × 6" deep

SKILL LEVEL Beginner ❀

MATERIALS

Amounts are based on 42"-wide fabric.

1⅛ yard for exterior

1⅛ yards for lining

⅛ yard contrasting fabric for handles (*optional*)

1¾ yards of fusible interfacing (*optional*)

¾" (18mm) magnetic snap

7" all-purpose zipper

NOTE
- A ⅜" seam allowance is included on the pattern.

- Backstitch at the beginning and end of each seam.

Valentina Bag

Draw the pattern directly onto the wrong side of a folded layer of fabric, or place the pattern on a single layer of fabric and draw around the shape as indicated on the pattern. Transfer all points and reference marks to the fabric. Cut out the exterior, lining, and interfacing.

Use the Valentina Bag Front and Back and Side patterns (pullout page P2).

Exterior

- 2 Front and Back pieces
- 2 Side pieces
- 1 piece 18¼″ × 6¾″ for Bottom
- 2 pieces 15″ × 4″ for handle (from the same fabric or optional contrasting fabric)

Lining

- 2 Front and Back pieces
- 2 Side pieces
- 1 piece 18½″ × 6¾″ for Bottom
- 2 pieces 7″ × 6″ for Lining Zipper Pocket
- 2 pieces 7″ × 5¾″ for Lining Pocket

Interfacing (optional)

- 2 Front and Back pieces
- 2 Side pieces
- 1 piece 18½″ × 6¾″ for Bottom
- 2 pieces 15″ × 4″ for handle

Applying the Magnetic Snap

Attach the magnetic snap onto the right side of the front and back lining pieces, following the manufacturer's instructions. See Applying a Magnetic Snap (page 9).

Sewing the Exterior

1. Fuse interfacing to the wrong side of the exterior pieces, following the manufacturer's instructions.

2. Place the exterior front and side pieces with right sides together. Pin and sew along the straight edges. Attach the other side piece to the front piece. Leave ⅜″ unsewn on each side at the bottom: This will make it easier to attach the side pieces to the bottom piece. **FIGURE A**

3. Pin and sew the exterior back piece to the exterior side pieces with right sides together, leaving ⅜″ unsewn at each end of the seam. **FIGURE B**

4. Pin and sew the exterior bottom piece to the front, back, and side pieces with right sides together, pivoting at each corner. Trim the corner seams at the bottom of the bag. **FIGURE C**

Sewing the Lining

1. Make and attach the pockets. See Standard Pocket (page 12) and Zipper Pocket (page 14). **FIGURE D**

2. Sew the lining pieces together in the same manner as the exterior, leaving a 6″ gap on 1 side at the bottom for turning. **FIGURE E**

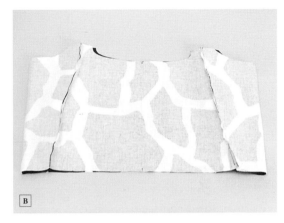

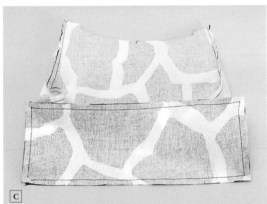

Stitching the Handles

1. Sew the handles. See Strap A (page 18). **FIGURE F**

2. Attach the handles by pinning and basting a raw end of each strap to the top edge of the front and back exterior pieces. **FIGURE G**

Assembling the Exterior and Lining

1. Press the exterior and lining seams open. Tuck the exterior into the lining with right sides together, sandwiching the handles between them. **FIGURE H**

2. Pin and sew the top opening of the exterior and lining pieces together, sewing over the attached handle and leaving an opening at the top end without a handle. **FIGURE I**

3. Clip the curved seam allowances and trim the corner seams. Turn the bag right side out through the lining opening. **FIGURE J**

4. Tuck in the top end seam and insert the handles into the opening and pin them in place.

5. Press the top seam and topstitch ⅛″ away from the edge around the top of the bag. **FIGURE K**

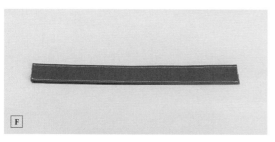

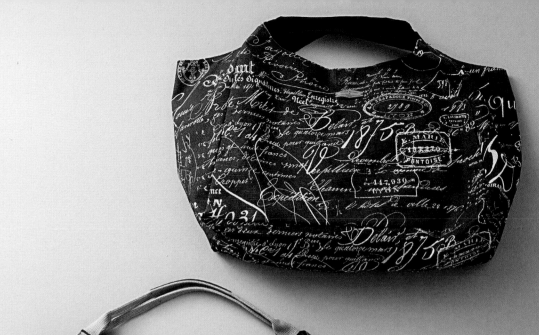

Valentina Bag

June Big Bag

The June Big Bag is just as its name implies, a roomy bag to handle all of your belongings for short outings or long vacations. The adjustable buckle provides comfort to alter the strap length. Recommended, but optional, ornaments that will enhance the bag further are items such as twist locks or buttons on the flap.

FINISHED SIZE 18½" wide × 13" high × 2" deep

SKILL LEVEL Confident Beginner

MATERIALS

Amounts are based on 42"-wide fabric.

1⅜ yards for exterior

1 yard for lining

1⅛ yards of fusible interfacing

16" all-purpose zipper for lining closing

7" all-purpose zipper for lining pocket

18mm magnetic snap or 2" twist locks/purse flip locks

1½" adjustable buckle

1½" lobster clasp

1½" D-ring

1 button, 2½" diameter (*optional, to use with magnetic snap*)

> **NOTE**
> - A ⅜" seam allowance is included on the pattern.
> - Backstitch at the beginning and end of each seam.

June Big Bag

CUTTING

Transfer all points and reference marks to the fabric. Cut out the exterior, lining, and interfacing.

Exterior

- 2 pieces 19¼″ × 13¾″ for Front and Back
- 2 pieces 2¾″ × 20¾″ for Gusset
- 1 piece 17¾″ × 13½″ for Flap
- 2 pieces 6″ × width of fabric for strap and loop

Lining

- 2 pieces 19¼″ × 13¾″ for Front and Back
- 2 pieces 2¾″ × 20¾″ for Gusset
- 1 piece 17¾″ × 13½″ for Flap
- 2 pieces 17½″ × 1¾″ for Lining Top Zipper Panel
- 2 pieces 7″ × 6″ for Lining Zipper Pocket

Interfacing

- 2 pieces 19¼″ × 13¾″ for Front and Back
- 2 pieces 2¾″ × 20¾″ for Gusset
- 1 piece 17¾″ × 13½″ for Flap

Refer to the Front and Back and Flap diagrams (at right) to trace and trim the bottom corners of all the Front and Back and Flap pieces using the June Big Bag Front and Back Corner and Flap Corner patterns (pullout page P1).

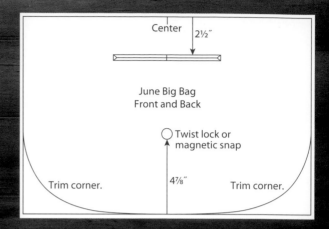

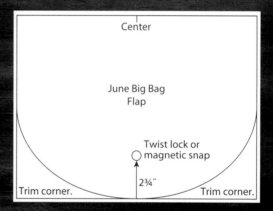

NOTE

- A ⅜″ seam allowance is included on the pattern.
- Backstitch at the beginning and end of each seam.

Sewing the Exterior

1. Fuse the interfacing to the wrong side of the exterior pieces, following the manufacturer's instructions.

2. Attach the bottom piece of the twist lock to the exterior front piece as indicated in the diagram. See Attaching a Twist Lock (page 11). If using the magnetic snap, attach it to the exterior front piece and the lining flap. See Applying a Magnetic Snap (page 9).

3. Place the gusset pieces with right sides together. Pin in place and stitch; press the seam open.

4. Pin the front piece to the assembled gusset piece with right sides facing. First, match the center front with the gusset seam, and then pin each end. Clip the gusset piece between the curved areas only as necessary to help ease it around the curve of the front piece.

5. Sew all around the front and gusset together. **FIGURE A**

6. Clip the curved seam. **FIGURE B**

7. Repeat Steps 4–6 to attach the back piece.

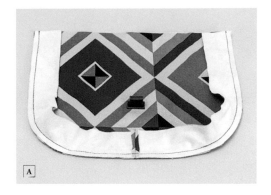

A

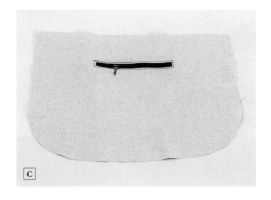

B

C

Making the Lining

1. Install the lining zipper pocket, 2½″ down from the top. See Zipper Pocket (page 14). **FIGURE C**

2. Make the lining. Repeat Steps 3–7 in Sewing the Exterior. Leave an opening for turning at the bottom. **FIGURE D**

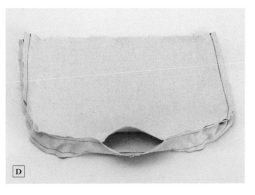

D

Attaching the Inside Zipper Panel

1. Close the zipper and lay it on the lining top zipper panel with right sides together. You will be able to see the wrong side of the zipper. Pin the zipper and panel in place. Stitch the zipper to the panel using a zipper foot. Begin sewing ¾″ from the end of the panel and stop ¾″ from the other end, sewing ¼″ from the zipper coil. Backstitch to secure. **FIGURE E**

2. Place the lining piece and the exterior piece with right sides together. The zipper will now be between the exterior and the lining.

3. Pin and stitch the 3 layers together close to the zipper coils, once again leaving ¾″ unstitched at each end. **FIGURE F**

4. Flip the lining over to the wrong side and press.

5. Repeat Steps 1–4 for the other exterior and lining pieces. **FIGURE G**

6. Fold the exterior edge seams inward ⅜″ at each end and press. Repeat for the lining. **FIGURE H**

7. Fold the long edges in ⅜″. Repeat for the lining. **FIGURE I**

8. Separate the zipper ends and push them into the zipper panels. Topstitch the zipper panel close to the zipper coils through all the layers. **FIGURES J & K**

9. Pin the zipper unit to the front and back of the lining bag, 1″ below the top edge. Stitch close to the folded edge. **FIGURE L**

E

F

G

H

I

J

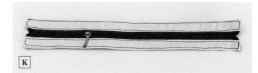

K

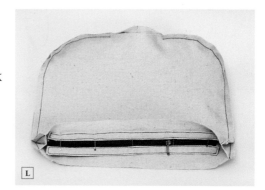

L

Stitching the Flap

1. Pin the exterior flap and lining flap with right sides facing. Stitch only the curved seam, leaving the straight edge unstitched. Notch the curved seam.

2. Turn the flap right side out and press.

3. Topstitch ½" from the edge. **FIGURE M**

4. Center the flap onto the back piece of the bag with exterior sides together, aligning the raw edges. Pin and baste in place. **FIGURE N**

5. Attach the front twist lock piece onto the flap. See Attaching a Twist Lock (page 11).

Stitching the Strap, Loop, and Handle

1. Sew the 2 strap pieces together at an end. Press the seam open. Cut 1 piece at 6" × 61½" for the strap and 1 piece at 6" × 11" for the ring loop.

2. Sew the strap. See Strap B (page 19).

3. Sew the ring loop. See Strap A (page 18). Insert an end of the ring loop through the D-ring and fold the loop in half. Pin the raw ends of the loop together to keep the D-ring from slipping out.

4. Center the raw end of the loop on the exterior gusset seam, with right sides together. Pin and baste in place.

5. Center the raw end of the strap on the other exterior side seam, with right sides together. Pin and baste in place. **FIGURE O**

Assembling the Exterior and Lining

1. Insert the exterior into the lining, right sides together. The flap, strap, and ring loops should be sandwiched between the lining and exterior.

2. Pin the exterior and lining together around the opening of the bag. **FIGURE P**

3. Stitch around the opening of the bag. Trim the corners at the top of the seams.

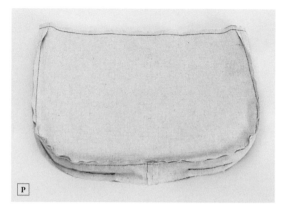

4. Turn the bag right side out through the opening in the lining. Stitch the opening closed. Tuck the lining into the exterior. Press the top opening of the bag. Topstitch around the opening ⅛″ from the edge.

5. Add the adjustable buckle. See Connecting an Adjustable Buckle (page 19). **FIGURE Q**

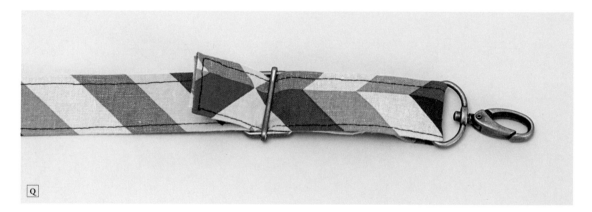

Miranda Bag

The Miranda Bag is an easy-to-make shopping bag with a simple kind of beauty. This bag has an overall loose form, which gives it a casual and comfortable feeling. As a result, it matches well with outfits of a similar relaxed style, such as a flowing sundress and flip-flops. The Miranda Bag is also ideal for taking along to the beach, as it is the perfect size to carry a light change of clothes, a swimsuit, and a towel.

FINISHED SIZE 20″ wide × 17″ high (without handle) × 3″ deep

SKILL LEVEL Beginner ❀

MATERIALS

Amounts are based on 42″-wide fabric.

1 yard for exterior

1 yard for lining

¾ yard of fusible interfacing

1 yard of 1¼″-wide of webbing (3cm width) or 1 set of 15″ leather/webbing handles

---

NOTE

• A ⅜″ seam allowance is included on the pattern.

• Backstitch at the beginning and end of each seam.

Transfer all points and reference marks to the fabric. Cut out the exterior, lining, and interfacing.

Use the Miranda Bag Front and Back Pleats Panel pattern (pullout page P2).

Exterior

- 4 pieces 15¾″ × 4¾″ for Front and Back Top
- 2 pieces 24¼″ × 15¼″ for Front and Back Pleats Panel

Lining

- 2 pieces 24¼″ × 15¼ for Front and Back Pleats Panel

Interfacing

- 4 pieces 15¾″ × 4¾″ for Front and Back Top

Webbing (if not using premade handles)

- 2 pieces 15″

Making the Exterior and Lining

1. Apply interfacing to the wrong side of the exterior front and back, following the manufacturer's instructions.

2. With the Front and Back Pleats Panel pattern, trace the pleats pattern onto the right side of a long edge of the fabric; then flip the pattern over and trace the second half. With the exterior front piece right side up, fold the pleats as indicated on the pattern, aligning it with the placement line, and pin. Repeat this process for all the pleats. **FIGURE A**

3. On the wrong side of the fabric, the pleats should be facing out. From the right side of the fabric, they should be facing in toward the center. Sew along each folded pleat, 3⅜″ down the fold. Backstitch on both ends. **FIGURE B**

4. Pin the center of the exterior front top piece to the pleated exterior front piece with right sides together. Then pin the rest of the top piece to the pleats. Stitch the 2 pieces together.

5. Flip the top piece right side up and press the seam. Topstitch ⅛″ away from the seam. Repeat Steps 4 and 5 for the exterior back piece. **FIGURE C**

6. Pleat the lining pieces in the same manner. After making the lining pleats, sew the lining pieces to the remaining exterior top pieces.

7. Place a webbing handle piece on the right side of the exterior front piece 2″ away from the center on each side. Pin and baste in place. Repeat for the exterior back piece. **FIGURE D**

8. Place the assembled exterior front and back pieces with right sides together. Smooth out the exterior pieces, so that the bottom of the fabric is flat. Pin along the edges. Make a mark 1½″ below the lower seam of the top piece on the edge of each piece. This is point A. Sew from the first point A around the bottom of the bag to the next point A. **FIGURE E**

9. Draw a 1½″ × 1½″ square on the bottom corners of the exterior, and cut away the square. **FIGURE F**

10. Push out the bottom corner and press it flat so that the edges meet and the corner forms a triangle. Pin and sew, ⅜″ from edge. Sew over the same seam 2–3 times to secure the corner. Repeat for the other corner. **FIGURE G**

11. Repeat Steps 8–10 for the lining. Leave a gap on the bottom to turn right side out.

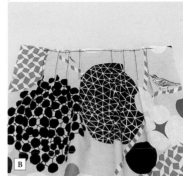

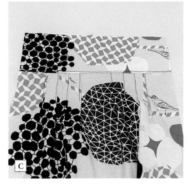

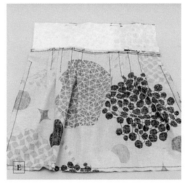

Miranda Bag

Assembling the Exterior and Lining

1. Turn the exterior right side out and tuck it into the lining with right sides together. The handles should be sandwiched between the layers. **FIGURE H**

2. Pin the exterior and lining front tops together. Sew around the top from a point A to the other. Sew the exterior and lining back tops together in the same manner. **FIGURE I**

3. Trim the corner seams. Notch the seams at point A. **FIGURE J**

4. Turn the bag right side out through the lining opening and stitch the opening closed.

5. Press and topstitch the opening of the bag. Start and end at the same point, pivoting at the corners and side seams. **FIGURE K**

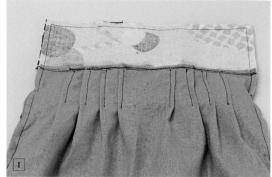

Miranda Bag

Stephanie Bag

The Stephanie Bag is designed to be the go-to bag for busy women. It is deep enough to carry all essential items. For those of you who have a hard time deciding on one fabric to use for your creations, there is an option to use seven different fabrics. The leather handles are hand-stitched to the bag and give the bag its unique feel. The patchwork and handle-attaching process takes a bit of work, but the final result is so rewarding that the extra effort is definitely worth it. Let's brighten up our day with this colorful, eye-catching bag!

FINISHED SIZE 12¼" wide × 14¼" high × 4½" deep (without handle)

SKILL LEVEL Beginner ❀

MATERIALS

Amounts are based on 42"-wide fabric.

⅝ yard for exterior (or ⅛ to ⅜ yard of 6 fabrics plus ½ yard for back for pieced option)

¾ yard for lining

1 yard of interfacing

Set of 21" leather handles

7" all-purpose zipper for lining zipper pocket

¾" (18mm) magnetic strap

> **NOTE**
> - A ¼" seam allowance is included on the pattern.
> - Backstitch at the beginning and end of each seam.

Stephanie Bag

CUTTING

Transfer all points and reference marks to the fabric. Cut out the exterior, lining, and interfacing.

Refer to the Front and Back diagram below to trace and trim the bottom corners of the exterior, lining, and interfacing using the Stephanie Bag Front and Back Corner pattern (pullout page P1).

Exterior

One-fabric front option

• 2 pieces 16″ × 17″ for Front and Back

Patchwork front option

• 1 piece 16″ × 4¼″ for Front (From Top)

• 1 piece 16″ × 1¾″ for Front

• 1 piece 16″ × 4¾″ for Front

• 1 piece 16″ × 2¾″ for Front

• 1 piece 16″ × 1¾″ for Front

• 1 piece 16″ × 4¼″ for Front

• 1 piece 16″ × 17″ for Back

Lining

• 2 Pieces 16″ × 17″ for Front and Back

• 2 Pieces 7″ × 6″ for Lining Zipper Pockets

Interfacing

• 2 pieces 16″ × 17″ for Front and Back

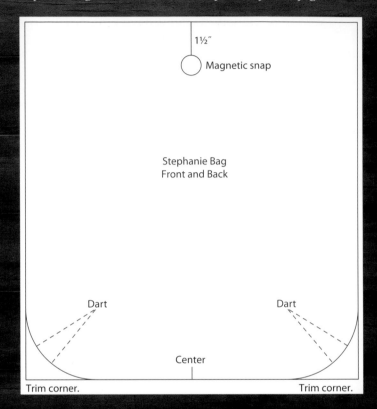

Sewing the Exterior Front Piece (*optional*)

Arrange the strips in the order given and sew together the strips using a ¼″ seam to make the exterior front piece. Press the seams to a side and topstitch each seam. If needed, trim to 16″ wide and 17″ tall. Trim bottom corners as noted in the Front and Back diagram (page 112).

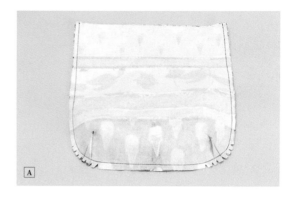

Sewing the Exterior and Lining

1. Fuse the interfacing to the wrong side of the exterior front and back, following the manufacturer's instructions.

2. Make the darts in the exterior and lining pieces. See Sewing Darts (page 17).

3. Place the exterior front and back pieces with right sides together. Pin and sew the exterior, making a U shape and backstitching both sides. The darts will face the opposite directions.

4. Clip the curved corner seams. **FIGURE A**

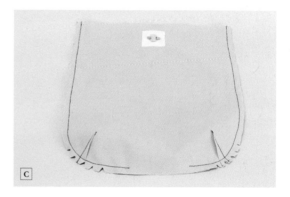

5. Install the lining zipper pocket 2¾″ down from the top. See Zipper Pocket (page 14).

6. Install the magnetic snap to the lining front and back. See Applying a Magnetic Snap (page 9). **FIGURE B**

7. Sew the lining front and back together as in Steps 1 and 2 above, leaving an opening at the bottom for turning. **FIGURE C**

Assembling the Exterior and Lining

1. Press the exterior and lining seams open. Turn the exterior right side out and tuck it into the lining with right sides together. **FIGURE D**

2. Pin and sew the exterior and lining pieces around the top opening of the bag. Turn the bag right side out through the opening and stitch the opening closed. **FIGURE E**

3. Tuck the lining into the exterior and press the top opening. Topstitch ⅛″ away from the seam. **FIGURE F**

Attaching the Handle

Place the handles on the exterior of the bag at the desired location. Follow the manufacturer's instructions to attach them. See Sewing a Leather and Webbing Handle (page 18).

Les doux flocons de
la neige ont disparu
silencieusem ent
dans tes mains

Stephanie Bag

Market Bag and Pouch

This project is suitable for all sewing levels. The large Market Bag easily

folds into the carrying pouch—how convenient. Keep the Market Bag

with you at all times for those fun shopping trips.

FINISHED SIZE 12″ wide × 16½″ high × 4½″ deep

SKILL LEVEL Beginner ❀

MATERIALS

Amounts are based on 42″-wide fabric.

1 yard for bag exterior (*optional: 2 fabrics pieced together for the front*)

¼ yard for pocket or individual pouch

1¼ yards for lining

¾″ (18mm) magnetic snap (*optional*)

5″ of narrow elastic for button closure

2 buttons, 1″ diameter

> **NOTE**
> You can follow the instructions for the pocket to make an individual pouch.

> **NOTE**
> - A ⅜″ seam allowance is included on the pattern.
> - Backstitch at the beginning and end of each seam.

CUTTING

Transfer all points and reference marks to the fabric. Cut out the exterior, pocket, and lining.

Use the Market Bag Front and Back, Pocket Front and Back, and Pocket Flap pattern (pullout page P1).

Draw the pattern directly onto the wrong side of a single layer of fabric. Transfer all points and reference marks to the fabric. Cut out the exterior, lining, and interfacing.

Exterior

- 2 Front and Back pieces
- 2 Pocket Front and Back pieces
- 1 Pocket Flap piece

Lining

- 2 Front and Back pieces
- 2 Pocket Front and Back pieces
- 1 Pocket Flap piece

Sewing the Exterior and Lining

1. Place the front and back pieces with right sides together, pin both sides, and stitch. Pin the bottom and stitch together. **FIGURE A**

2. Match the side and bottom seams with right sides together. Pin in place and stitch. Repeat this process for the other side. **FIGURE B**

3. Attach the magnetic snap onto the lining pieces 2″ down from the top and centered. See Applying a Magnetic Snap (page 9). **FIGURE C**

4. Sew the lining pieces together like Steps 1 and 2 above. Leave a 6″ opening for turning.

Assembling the Exterior and Lining

1. Turn the exterior right side out and tuck it into the lining with right sides together. **FIGURE D**

2. Pin the exterior and lining pieces together at the curved seam from the top of a handle to the top of the other handle. Sew, leaving the top 2″ of the handles unsewn. Then pin each of the remaining curves and sew in the same manner. **FIGURE E**

3. Clip the inside corner seam allowances and trim the corner seams. **FIGURE F**

4. Turn the bag right side out through the bottom opening. Sew the opening closed.

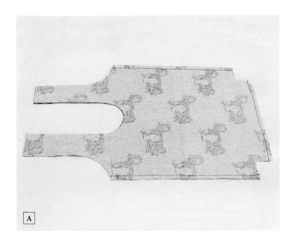

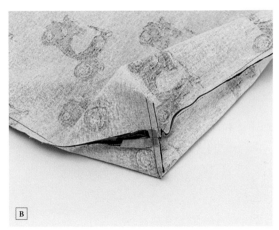

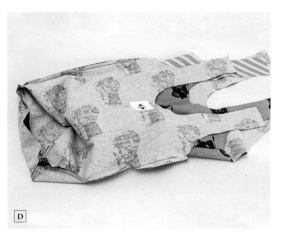

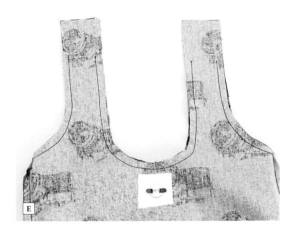

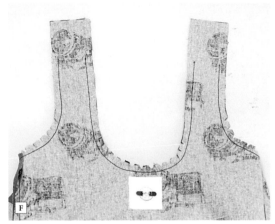

Market Bag and Pouch

Constructing the Handle

1. Tuck the lining into the exterior. Place the exterior handles with right sides together. Pin and sew together along the short edges. Press the seam open. Repeat this process for the lining. **FIGURE G**

2. Tuck in the raw edges of the seam allowances on both sides of the straps and press. **FIGURE H**

3. Pin or baste the strap opening. Topstitch ⅛" away from the seam around the armhole of the bag. Topstitch the other armhole and the main opening of the bag. **FIGURE I**

Making the Pocket or Pouch

Making the Front and Back

1. Place the front and back pieces with right sides together. Sew around the exterior front and back. Clip the curves. **FIGURE J**

2. Repeat this process for the lining.

G

H

I

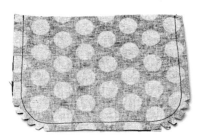

J

Making the Flap

1. Place the elastic loop onto the exterior flap, facing in, and baste in place. **FIGURE K**

2. Pin the exterior flap and lining flap with right sides facing. Stitch only the rounded seam, leaving a straight edge unstitched for turning. Clip the curved seam. **FIGURE L**

3. Turn the flap right side out. Press the flap; topstitch ¼″ away from the curved seam only. **FIGURE M**

4. Place the flap onto the back of the pocket exterior with exterior sides facing, aligning the raw edge of the pocket and the flap. Pin and baste the flap to the pocket. **FIGURE N**

K

L

M

N

Assembling the Pocket Exterior and Lining

1. Press the exterior and lining seams open. Put the exterior into the lining with right sides together, sandwiching the flap between the exterior and the lining. **FIGURE O**

2. Pin the opening of the pocket. Sew along the opening of the pocket using a ⅜″ seam allowance, leaving a 3″ gap to turn it right side out. **FIGURE P**

O

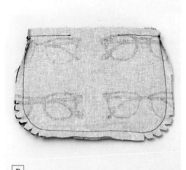

P

3. Trim the corner seams. Turn the pocket right side out. Iron the opening of the pocket. Tuck the lining into the exterior. Topstitch all around the opening of the pocket. **FIGURE Q**

4. Turn the pocket inside out and sew the button to the lining front. Turn the pocket right side out and sew the optional second button to the front.

5. Attach the pocket onto the bag 4″ down from the center top. Pin in place and stitch together at the top of the back. **FIGURE R**

Folding the Bag

1. Fold the sides toward the center, beneath the pocket. **FIGURE S**

2. Flip the bag on its back. Fold the handles and the bottom up toward the center. **FIGURE T**

3. Turn the pocket inside out while inserting the bag into the pocket. **FIGURE U**

4. Hook the elastic around the button. **FIGURE V**

Q

R

S

T

U

V

Market Bag and Pouch

Gallery

Julianna Bag and Madison Metal Coin Case

Violet Bag and Evelyn Clutch

Stephanie Bag and Jayleen Clutch, oilcloth fabric

Madison Metal Purse, silk fabric   *Madison Metal Purse, embellished fabric*   *Madison Metal Purse, metallic fabric*

Thelma Bag, metallic fabric

Susan Boston Bag, Madison Metal Purse, and Gathered Zipper Pouches

Jayleen Clutch, faux leather

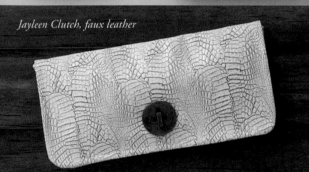

Violet Bag and Linnea Ruffled Bag, lace fabric

Jayleen Clutch, beaded fabric

About the Author

Sue Kim lives in Manitoba, Canada, with her three lovely children and husband. You may find her latest designs on her website, ithinksew.com. She started sewing when she was ten years old and has always had a passion for crafts. She earned a master's degree in ancient Asian literature. However, she kept sewing and designing as a hobby until luckily she was asked to be a sewing instructor at a Jo-Ann Fabric and Crafts store. That expanded into requests to instruct in several quilt shops; the quilt shop owners also encouraged her to start her own pattern business. Her first patterns were for small bags and clutches, and eventually she was asked to make a pattern book on bags and clutches! Now, most of the patterns Sue sells are downloadable PDF patterns rather than printed patterns. She has completed several books of patterns and has become an independent pattern designer who is now writing for several publishers and pattern companies.

Resources

Riley Blake
rileyblakedesigns.com

Fat Quarter Shop
fatquartershop.com

Cloud 9 Fabric
cloud9fabrics.com

Sue Kim's Fabric
spoonflower.com/profiles/ithinksew